QP   Corrick, James A.
376
.C658 The human brain
1983

THE
HUMAN BRAIN

THE**ARCO** HOW IT WORKS SERIES

THE
HUMAN BRAIN
• MIND AND MATTER •

JAMES A. CORRICK

**ARCO PUBLISHING, INC.
NEW YORK**

56347

MAY 3 1 1984

Published by Arco Publishing, Inc.
215 Park Avenue South, New York, N.Y. 10003

Library of Congress Cataloging in Publication Data

Corrick, James A.
  The human brain.

  (The Arco how-it-works series)
  Includes index.
  Summary: Explores such topics as intelligence and
memory, sleep, brain waves, right/left coordination,
pain, biofeedback, phrenology, memory transplants,
psychic powers, and brain research and technology.
  1. Brain—Juvenile literature. [1. Brain]
I. Title. II. Series: Arco how-it-works series.
QP376.C658 1983   612'.82   82-18461
ISBN 0-668-05519-7

Printed in the United States of America

10 9 8 7 6 5 4 3 2 1

To my father and mother,
who always encouraged me to write

Contents

Acknowledgments

I should particularly like to thank the following people for their time and effort in supplying me with information and materials for this book. Without their help, this would have been a far poorer book.

Naturally, any errors or mistakes in the text are not the responsibility of these people, but are solely my own.

Jeffery Barker, Chief of the Laboratory of Neurophysiology at the National Institute of Neurological and Communicative Disorders and Stroke; Gayle Brucker of Telesensory Systems Inc.; Carter Collins of the Smith-Kettlewell Institute of Visual Sciences; Michael Crabtree, ECAT Scanner Program Manager for EG&G Ortec; Alan Gevins, Director of EEG Systems Laboratory; John Eric Holmes, Department of Neurology, University of Southern California School of Medicine; David Hubel of Harvard Medical School; Norman Komar of Tucson Medical Center; Diane McGuinness, Department of Psychology, Stanford University; William Masland of Neurological Associates; Charles Needham of Neurological Associates; András Pellionisz of New York University Medical Center; Michael Phelps, Division of Biophysics, University of California at Los Angeles; Carol Redvanly, Brookhaven National Laboratory; Joel Sugarman, Information Specialist, National Eye Institute; Barbara Tait, Nicolet Instruments; Michael Ter-Pogossian, College of Medicine, Washington University; Lynn Trible, Office of Scientific and Health Reports, National Institute of Neurological and Communicative Disorders and Stroke.

And finally, Gay Miller, who did not only the illustrations, but also much of the legwork in the final days.

Introduction

Think back a moment to the first manned flight of the space shuttle *Columbia*. NASA, the press, everyone was ready and willing to explain in great detail why the space shuttle was the most complicated machine ever designed to fly. But what was the most complicated system aboard the *Columbia*?

If you had asked any of the millions of viewers of the launch, you would have heard some say the onboard computer system. Others, the guidance system. Still others, the protective tiles.

Yet, it was none of these. Complex as these systems are and representing as they do a pinnacle of technology, they were and are eclipsed by a much older and infinitely more sophisticated system as old as the human species.

What is this system and where is it? It is the human brain. And in the case of the shuttle, it was the skulls of the two human pilots, John Young and Robert Crippen.

The human brain is a system? Indeed, yes. Although the brain is an organ, we are not talking about a heart or a liver, each of which does one thing. The brain does many things, performing more functions than the largest computer. It keeps the heart beating and the lungs pumping. It keeps us from falling down, tells us when we are hungry or cold, and lets us know when we have cut a finger or bruised an arm. It shows us the world through our eyes. It thinks through problems. It learns and remembers.

How does it do all this and much more? Well, no one has the complete answer to that, but scientists and researchers look at the brain and see systems that coordinate with one another so the brain can handle all the things we require of it. The elements of this system we call the brain are electrical and chemical. The researcher also looks at the brain as a system because it is so very complex. As Dr. Jeffery Barker, of the National Institute of Neurological and Communicative Disorders and Stroke, observes, "The functional complexity of the brain is very difficult to understand when the entire nervous system is considered. So, we look at systems or regions."

What do you know about the brain? Probably some vague facts. Most of the time, you probably do not think about it at all. Indeed, because of TV ads for antacids, you may be more aware of your stomach than of your brain. Until recently, even the specialists—the biologists, the doctors, the neurologists, and the biochemists—could tell us little about the brain and its operation. Only a quarter of a century ago, you would have been told by these scientists that they would need ten years to map and study an area of the brain's surface the size of a postage stamp. Because of these difficulties in studying the brain, more than one researcher of this period felt that the brain was the final frontier. But the technology of brain research exploded in the 60's and 70's. The age of the SST and the space shuttle had reached the biological sciences, and the study of the brain shot forward with the rapidity of a Japanese high-speed train. Microelectrodes fed information into computers so that the neurobiologist could examine smaller and smaller regions of the brain. Single nerve cells became the focus of study, so that Hubel and Wiesel could begin tracing the path of vision through the brain. Scientists, using radioactive tracers and the positron emission transaxial tomography (PETT) scanner, are now observing and mapping the chemical activity of the brain's various regions.

Nor do scientists merely study small regions of the brain. With new methods of mathematical analysis and computer assistance, electroencephalogram (EEG) operators can now watch the whole brain work at a single task. That single postage stamp has now become a whole sheet of stamps.

But where does all this research lead? To a better today? Perhaps. To a better tomorrow? Certainly. Drugless pain relief is coming as we learn more about endorphins, natural painkillers manufactured by our brains. Cures for stroke and Parkinson's disease will be done through transplantation of nerve cells. Elimination of blindness and deafness will come through a better understanding of how our senses work. What was a frontier of discovery has become a frontier of action.

And the more distant future? How would you like to have your own personal computer? Not, as you can now, a unit that plugs into your wall. Instead, one that will ride in your skull and connect directly into your brain so that whatever it knows you would know. Eventually the day will come when we will be able to control our memories, our ability to learn, and our very dreams. We will use the brain to correct faults not only in our bodies, but also in the brain's own functioning.

INTRODUCTION

By understanding our brains, we not only satisfy what Dr. David Hubel of the Harvard Medical School calls our "simple curiosity, the same reason why an astronomer looks at the sky," but also we come to understand ourselves and our relationship to the world better. According to Jeffery Barker, "We have to figure out how the brain functions. It's like figuring out ourselves, coming to grips with whom we have become. I am sure that, through understanding brain function, we will come to a better understanding of the society we have become."

The future is in the brain. So, let's go there.

THE
HUMAN BRAIN

1

Tracing the Labyrinth: The Basics of the Brain

The overhead fluorescents shine almost coldly on the stainless steel. The patient lies quietly on the padded table. Behind glass panels in a dimly lit room sit the doctors and technicians. Suddenly, the table begins to slide slowly forward. Its destination is a large rectangular box in the center of which is an opening. The table stops when the patient's head is within the opening. Nothing happens. At least not in the room with the box and the patient.

However, within the glass-paneled room, a control console, as imposing as a section of Mission Control in the Manned Space Center at Houston, comes to life. Readings march across TV screens, recorders click and whir, buttons and levers are set and reset. Most spectacular are the TV screens that show the shifting reds, yellows, and blues. At first, they seem almost meaningless. But the trained doctors see them as a picture of one section of the patient's brain. They watch for some thirty minutes as the colors shift and merge in an ever-changing but ever-revealing pattern of brain activity.

Now they know what is wrong with their patient. These medical professionals are using one of the newest and most useful brain research tools, the PETT (Positron Emission Transaxial Tomography) scanner.

But before we can talk about this and the other modern tools of the brain researchers, we must first learn something about the parts of the brain. We can't talk about the instruments until we know what they are studying. We must become familiar with the cerebrum, the cerebellum, the neuron, and many other parts of our brain and our nervous system to understand the research not only of today, but of yesterday.

Not everything about the brain is exciting. Watching it isn't. Bad science-fiction movies often show the living human brain as a throbbing, pulsing blob that sometimes gives off light. Nothing of the kind happens. If you could watch the working brain, you would be disappointed. Unlike the beating heart or the pumping lungs, the brain is physically quiet. True, blood circulates through the various arteries, veins, and capillaries of the brain, but blood moves in all parts of the body and is driven by the heart.

The Brain's Invisible Activity

The brain's activity is not visible to the unaided human eye. But then neither are the microscopic creatures in a drop of water. Yet, these animals and plants move, live, and die with all the drama of their gigantic cousins. When we walk along the streets of our neighborhood, we occasionally look up and see the power and telephone lines that connect the houses. We can't see the activity in them, but we know it is there. They carry current from the generating stations to the houses, they relay hundreds of phone calls around the nearby blocks. Just as with the brain, this activity is invisible.

Our failure to see the brain's activity means little. The firing of nerve cells is constant. Chemicals move from cell to cell, from region to region in an endless dance of work. Maybe we can't see all this, but in one sense we can watch the brain work. All we need do is watch our own bodies operate.

Imagine you are sitting with a friend, trying to decide what movie to see that night. Your friend explains why he wants to see *Grease II*. Your ears catch the sound of his words and route them to the hearing center of your brain. Your brain analyzes these words, fitting them into your own arguments for going to see *Blade Runner*. Your brain then sends signals from your speech center to your vocal cords and tongue so you can tell your friend your reasoning.

Seems simple enough, but this is far from everything the brain is doing while you two talk. Through your eyes, the brain is monitoring your friend's facial expressions and body movement. Is his mouth turning down; is he tapping his fingers on his chair arm? You are losing the argument. The brain changes strategy. Meanwhile, the brain also sees everything else in your field of vision: the lamp with its crooked shade, the slightly frayed carpet, a framed picture hanging on the wall behind your friend's head. Little of this registers in your conscious mind. The brain, however, keeps you from being drowned in too much sensory information. It constantly acts as a clearinghouse to tell you what is and what is not important.

But we are not through. To keep you from falling out of your chair, the brain is also adjusting and readjusting your balance. It shifts your body to avoid that broken spring, but stops you long before you slide off the chair's end. On another level, it takes care of your body's housework. It sees that the liver filters your blood and that those corn chips you just ate get digested. And there are a thousand other activities it is performing during this brief conversation. Think what it must be doing when you are running. At no time, day or night, even when the body is asleep, is the brain inactive.

The brain is your own personal air traffic control center. In a traffic control center, each controller deals with several airplanes at once. He or she watches the flight pattern of each plane as that pattern relates to that of other planes on the controller's scope. The entire center handles dozens of planes at once. In the brain, each region is like that traffic control center. Each center is responsible for monitoring and controlling the body's various parts and actions. All of these centers communicate with one another so that the brain can function as a unit. We could, with a little stretching, compare the nerve cells of the brain, the neurons, to the individual controllers.

Brain Structure

If the brain's functioning is complex, its structure is equally complicated. The brain has three major parts: the *cerebrum*, the *cerebellum*, and the *brain stem*. Each of these in turn have numerous regions that control specific functions and are still in the process of being mapped by researchers. Just how many divisions the brain actually has is still a matter of question, but the major operations of the three sections of the brain have been well established for years.

Looking at Figures 1 and 2, diagrams of the human brain, we see that the cerebrum is the largest of the three parts. It envelops and surrounds the upper portion of the brain stem, almost seeming to grow out of it. The cerebellum nestles between the rear section of the cerebrum and the brain stem. The lower half of the brain stem connects the brain with the spinal cord. The brain is really nothing more than an enlargement of the upper end of the spinal cord. The brain may be part of the spinal cord, but it weighs three pounds

Figure 1.   Side view of the human brain.

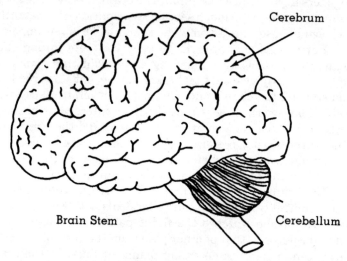

Cerebrum

Brain Stem   Cerebellum

*Figure 2.   Cross section of the brain within the skull. Notice that the position-
ing of cerebrum, cerebellum, and brain stem are different from those in
Figure 1.*

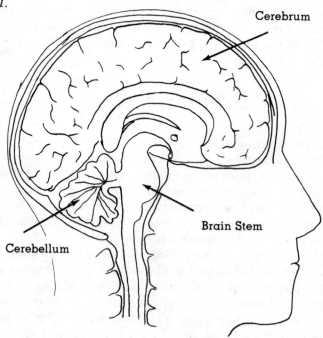

Cerebrum

Brain Stem

Cerebellum

compared to the entire spinal cord's half a pound. This difference doesn't mean the spinal cord isn't important, but it does tell us where to find the vast majority of the nervous system's operations, in that overswollen end, the brain.

The Well-Protected Brain

Anything as important as the brain is well protected. Like the president of the United States, the brain has its own secret service. From the outside, you can see only the first barrier between brain and damage, the skull. The brain is the only organ in the body completely encased in bone. If the skull were the only protection, however, the brain would be in almost as much danger from the skull as, say, a blow from a club. Any movement would hurl the soft, spongy brain against hard bone, causing serious injury. So, a second line of defense stands between brain and skull: three membranes that act as cushions. The outermost of these membranes is the *dura mater,* meaning "hard mother," and it is composed of hard fibers. The second layer is the *arachnoid membrane,* which is as web-like as its spidery name implies. Finally, the third membrane is the *pia mater,* the "soft mother," which tightly covers the surface of the brain much like a very snug stocking.

The brain's defense is completed by a third protector: the *cerebrospinal fluid.* The brain—like a baby in a womb—floats constantly in this fluid, which provides a final cushion, acting along with the membranes to keep the brain from smashing into the bone of the skull. The brain also needs the cerebrospinal fluid to maintain its shape. Without this fluid, the brain would be crushed down into the lower part of the skull by the pull of gravity.

The protective system of the brain is elaborate but ingenious. And it is absolutely essential.

The Cerebrum

If you looked at a specimen of the human brain, you would see that the *cerebrum,* in Latin meaning simply "the brain," dominates the other parts of the brain. From the top (see Figure 3), you see nothing else.

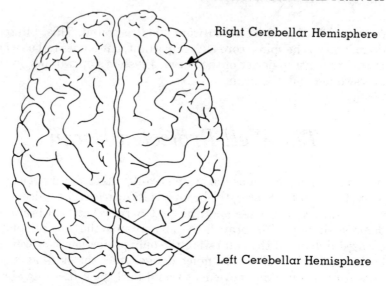

Right Cerebellar Hemisphere

Left Cerebellar Hemisphere

Figure 3.   Top view of the human brain.

Figure 4.   Bottom view of the human brain.

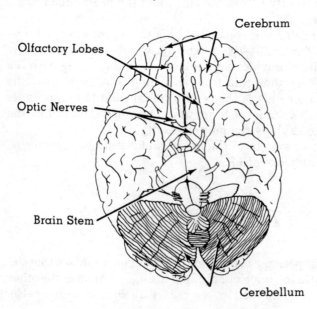

Cerebrum

Olfactory Lobes

Optic Nerves

Brain Stem

Cerebellum

And even from below (see Figure 4), where the cerebellum and the brain stem are most visible, the cerebrum looms above and around them much as an aerial balloon overshadows its gondola. Of the brain's mass, the cerebrum accounts for over eighty percent.

The gray surface of the cerebrum is wrinkled and furrowed. These furrows vary in depth. The deepest are called fissures and are used to mark the borders between different sections of the cerebrum. One particularly large fissure runs from the front to the back (see Figure 3) of the cerebrum; the two halves are called the *cerebral hemispheres*. This surface, which is a few centimeters deep, is called the *cortex*, meaning bark or rind. Much of the activity so far studied is located in this outermost layer of the cerebrum. Major sections of the cerebral hemispheres are named for the bones of the skull under which they lie. Thus, the upper front of the hemispheres are the frontal lobes (see Figure 5), on the side are the temporal lobes, and in the back, the parietal and occipital lobes.

The furrowing of the cerebral cortex increases the surface area of the cerebrum, for the surface area of these grooves is twice that found on the ridges between. If the cerebrum were smooth, the brain would have to be two and a half to three times as large as it is now. To understand why, take a sheet of paper and fold it accordion-fashion. It still has the same amount of area, but it looks smaller. Without a similar folding of the brain, the human head would have to be much larger. No female could give birth to any child with a head of that size since her pelvis would be far too small. So, the old science-fiction idea

Figure 5. Cerebrum.

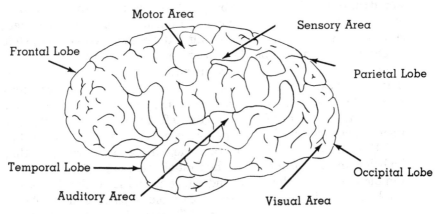

of the human race evolving into a species with large heads and small bodies is physically impossible.

The cerebrum is so large so it can handle the great number of operations that this section of the brain controls. Intelligence and memory are both functions of the cerebrum. Damage to the parts of the cerebrum can interfere with the reasoning and remembering processes. Additionally, speech and hand movement, both linked very closely with the development of human intelligence, are controlled by centers in the cerebrum.

Besides regulating the muscles of the hand, the cerebrum also governs muscular movement for the rest of the body. The motor area occupies the upper middle half of the cerebral cortex, just behind the frontal lobes (see Figure 5). The brain sometimes seems to have a logic of its own, divorced from what we would expect. In the motor area, the top controls the legs and feet, not the head. The head is directed by the lowest level of this section. The brain's perverse logic continues when we look for the vision center. It's not in the front of the cerebrum, but in the rear, at the back of the occipital lobes. Moreover, the optic nerve that runs from the eye to the brain does not run to the visual cortex. Rather it enters the brain stem. We shall see something more of its convoluted path into the rest of the brain in Chapter 4.

Just below the motor area, running along the top of the temporal lobe, is the auditory area. The sensory area, which registers touches on the skin, runs up from the auditory area alongside the motor area. Like the motor area, the sensory receives signals from the legs at the top and from the head at the bottom. In some ways, the brain is almost like a photographic negative, and the body like the positive print.

Logically, we might expect that the two cerebral hemispheres would control their respective body halves. But the brain again operates with its own logic. For some reason, which no one yet understands, the nerves from the right half of the body cross over to the left cerebral hemisphere, and those from the left half of the body go to the right hemisphere. Between the two hemispheres is a bridge of nerve fibers called the *corpus callosum* (see Figure 6). The two hemispheres keep in touch with each other and coordinate their activity through this bridge. Without it, the left hand would literally not know what the right hand is doing (as we shall see in Chapter 3).

Hidden from view by the brain stem are several structures that lie below the cerebral cortex. The first of these is the *limbic system.* Limbic means "border," and indeed, it is the lower border of the cerebrum. The limbic system is one of the oldest parts of the cerebrum and is sometimes called the old brain. The remainder of the cerebrum

THE MISSING CEREBRUM

A major element in much scientific research is surprise. The expected is often not there, and the unexpected just as often appears. Sometimes even the most basic assumptions come under question. One such assumption is the conviction of most brain researchers that intelligence, learning, and memory are all functions strictly limited to the cerebrum. John Lorber of Sheffield University in England, however, has recently challenged this belief. Lorber has been studying people whose skulls have contained an excess of cerebrospinal fluid since birth. Because the cerebrospinal fluid takes up so much room in their skulls, it often retards the full development of the cerebrum. Thus, for these people, the upper portions of the cerebrum are missing.

If the cerebrum is, as has been generally supposed, the site of intelligence, learning, and memory, the people in Lorber's study should show below-normal intelligence and have problems learning and remembering, yet according to Lorber, no such problems exist for these people. Indeed, several show quite high I.Q.'s and function no differently than anyone else. One of those studied was a hospital worker with an I.Q. of 120; another, with an I.Q. of 126, held an honors degree in mathematics. Lorber feels that the lower brain structures, such as the brain stem, may have more to do with intelligence than researchers have always believed. Since the cerebrum, however, is not completely missing in these people, Lorber concedes that the functions of the cerebral hemispheres may possibly require only a small section of the cerebrum.

Perhaps many of the cells in the cerebrum, much like the back-up computers in the space shuttle, merely act as an emergency system. This system may take over in case of injury to the primary cells.

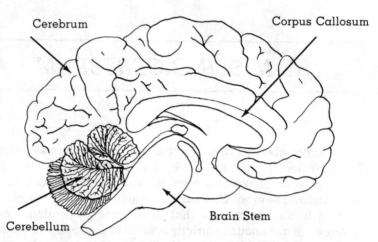

Figure 6.   Cross section of the human brain.

evolved along with our mammalian ancestors after the limbic system had developed. Sometimes called the visceral brain, the limbic system concerns itself with our various emotional responses, particularly hunger and sex. Have a craving for pizza? Blame your limbic system. Strangely enough, it also has a role in the process of learning.

The limbic system surrounds the *thalamus,* which comes from a Greek word meaning "room" (the Romans thought that this structure was an unfilled space). The thalamus responds primarily to signals of pain, heat, and cold. It acts as a filter for the sensory area of the cerebrum, allowing moderate temperatures and light, nonpainful touches to pass through to the upper region of the brain. Extremes of temperature and pain, anything requiring immediate attention, bring an almost automatic response from the thalamus.

Just below the thalamus is the hypothalamus, which means, appropriately enough, "beneath the thalamus." The hypothalamus controls a number of functions. It is our pleasure center. When we enjoy a drink or enjoy skiing, we do so because the pleasure center in our hypothalamus is stimulated. Just as our homes have thermostats, so our bodies have them as well. That thermostat is the hypothalamus. When our house becomes too cold in the winter, the thermostat turns on the furnace. When our bodies become too cold, our hypothalamus starts our muscles quivering to generate heat. If we become too hot, it triggers our sweat glands. A third important function of the hypothalamus is the control of waking and sleeping. Damage to the hypothalamus, such as swelling of brain tissue due to disease, can result in long periods of sleep, sometimes lasting years.

ST. VITUS AND PARKINSON'S

America is a dancing culture—at least, we like to think of ourselves as such. Dancing is featured in movies such as *Saturday Night Fever* and *Urban Cowboy*, and dance fads from the Charleston to the Twist to Country Swing are a part of our lives. Yet we cannot compare to medieval Europe where whole villages and towns were seized with fits of manic dancing. Although the underlying causes of these dances were psychological—a reaction against poor living conditions and the constant fear of plague and famine—the immediate spark may have been the sight of someone suffering from St. Vitus's dance.

A person with St. Vitus's dance appears to be dancing very clumsily and very jerkily. During the Middle Ages, a pilgrimage to the shrine of St. Vitus supposedly cured the disease. Actually, the problem generally clears up by itself. The cause of St. Vitus is an injury to the lower cerebrum. The nerve fibers controlling body movement and conveying sensory information pass through the limbic system, and any damage in this region can affect the impulses the brain sends to the body's muscles and bring about a loss of feeling in parts of the body. In St. Vitus's dance, this injury, which can be caused by rheumatic fever for instance, causes the muscles of the legs and arms to pull and jerk automatically.

A much more serious ailment from injury to the lower area of the cerebrum is Parkinson's disease. Injury to nerve fibers controlling body movement and sensory input results in Parkinson's disease. Sufferers from this disease develop over a period of years a gentle but constant twitching of the hands and head and an almost unnatural immobility of the face and arms. Thus the constant movement of head and hands makes a strange contrast to the mask-like face and stiffly held arms. Parkinson's disease takes years to reach its full extent, and, with medication, those afflicted can function normally for even longer. Thus when Representative Morris Udall of Arizona announced during the 1980 election that he had Parkinson's disease, no one, including his opponent, felt that it should keep him from being reelected.

THE SACRED DISEASE

We all have things we are afraid of, and we of the twentieth century are particularly adept at creating new fears from nuclear warfare to possible ecological collapse. Yet many of our fears are as old as the species. One of those fears is epilepsy, meaning seizure. However, the fear of having an epileptic fit is not so great as the fear of being around someone who has such a seizure. We think of uncontrollably thrashing bodies, frothing mouths, and bitten tongues. Although one form of epilepsy, known as *grand mal*, the "great sickness," approximates this image, it is not nearly so bad as we fear. Indeed, most attacks of epilepsy are comparatively mild, and the other major form, the *petit mal*, the "little sickness," is marked not by a physical attack, but sometimes by short periods of unconsciousness.

For the epileptic, the neurons in either the motor area, which controls the muscles of the body, or the sensory area, which receives and acts upon information from the eyes, nose, ears, etc., of the cerebrum, activate suddenly without any stimulus from other neurons. In some cases, this activity is caused by brain injury before birth or during childhood; in many cases, however, no cause for the activation can be found. Because the *grand mal* form of epilepsy is often so dramatic, epilepsy has been noted and remarked upon over a long stretch of human history. Such people as Alexander the Great, Julius Caesar, Lord Byron, and Vincent van Gogh were epileptics. However, the characteristics of the *grand mal* with its shaking and jerking and of the *petit mal* with its loss of consciousness have been seen in the past as forms of supernatural possession or demonic attacks. The Greeks saw the symptoms of epilepsy as signs of the gods taking over and speaking through the person affected; thus, for them, epilepsy was the sacred disease. The Delphic oracle was more believable as a prophet when she shook with an epileptic fit or faked epileptic attack. Modern mediums still shake and writhe when they supposedly contact the spirit world.

Hippocrates, originator of the Hippocratic Oath that modern doctors take, was the first to see that epilepsy was a disease and should be treated as such. In the twentieth century, much research has been done and continues to be done on epilepsy. Most sufferers of this disorder lead normal lives and are not recognized by most of us as epileptics, whether they play professional baseball or are corporate lawyers.

Soldiers who have been wounded in the hypothalamus, however, have sometimes found themselves unable to sleep again.

The Brain Stem

Like the stalk of a bent mushroom, the brain stem angles down and out from the cerebrum. Like the whole brain, the brain stem is also divided into three parts (see Figure 7): the *midbrain*; the *pons,* meaning "bridge"; and the *medulla oblongata,* Latin for "rather long marrow." Together, these divisions serve to regulate unconscious muscle activity.

When you go to a party, you spend your time moving around, talking with this person for a while, listening in on that group's

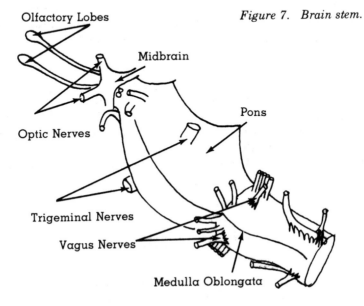

Olfactory Lobes

Figure 7. Brain stem.

Midbrain

Pons

Optic Nerves

Trigeminal Nerves

Vagus Nerves

Medulla Oblongata

conversation. You do not, however, think consciously of the process that keeps your body standing or walking. You think about the party. Yet the very complicated acts of standing and walking and the interplay between muscles to keep you balanced while walking or standing never require conscious control on your part. And if you think walking and standing are simple, just watch a baby trying to learn to do them. The brain stem automatically oversees and monitors these muscular interactions. When you first learn as a child to stand and walk, you must consciously think about what you are doing. As the act becomes more familiar, however, your brain stem takes over.

The brain stem is also a multiple electric socket into which nerves from the body to the brain plug in. Of the body's forty-three nerves, twelve go to the brain. Of these twelve, eleven end in the brain stem. The *olfactory nerve* goes directly to the cerebrum, which originally in mammals was involved strictly with smell.

The midbrain receives the optic nerve and most of the nerves that are connected with the muscles of the eye. The signal from the optic nerve, as we have seen, is routed from the midbrain to the cerebrum.

The nerves from the face end at the pons. The largest of these and the largest of the cranial nerves is the *trigeminal nerve*. Since the trigeminal has both sensory and motor fibers, it is called a mixed nerve.

One of the most important nerves in the body is the *vagus nerve,* another mixed nerve that sends impulses from the medulla oblongata to the heart and lungs. Damage this nerve, or the medulla oblongata, and the result is death. Through this nerve, this part of the brain stem also controls the digestive tract.

At the point where the pons and medulla oblongata join, the *stato-acoustic nerve,* which runs from the inner ear, connects with the brain stem. This nerve transmits sound impulses and also information about the body's balance, one of the inner ear's functions. Injury to this nerve or to this part of the brain stem can mean not only problems in hearing, but problems in keeping your equilibrium when standing, walking, or even sitting.

The Cerebellum

If the brain stem looks a little like a mushroom stalk, then the cerebellum resembles a snail clinging to that stalk just below the

Left Cerebral Hemisphere

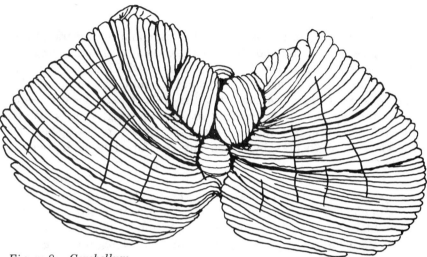

Figure 8. Cerebellum.

Right Cerebral Hemisphere

mushroom cap, the cerebrum. The cerebellum also looks like a smaller version of the cerebrum. Like this larger brain section, it is divided into two halves, the cerebellar hemispheres, and has furrows in its cortex (see Figure 8). This resemblance accounts for the cerebellum's name, which in Latin means "little brain."

The cerebellum, however, is not some sort of emergency backup for the cerebrum. Neither has any functions in common to anyone's knowledge. Instead, this "little brain" controls muscular coordination. When you reach for a pencil or a glass, you rarely overshoot or undershoot your mark. Your hand closes around the pencil or glass, lifting it back to you. You aren't even surprised at the ease and accuracy of your reach. You don't even think about it. But your brain does, and the cerebellum makes sure your unconscious confidence is justified. To lift a pencil or a glass of water, the muscles of your hand and arm must work together, often in partnership with your eyes. If they do not, you will have difficulty. A damaged or diseased cerebellum causes a person to grope around for that pencil. Unable to reach directly for it, a person may put his hand down either in front of or in back of the pencil. The simple act of drinking from a glass of water also requires the coordination supplied by the cerebellum. Without such coordination the muscles in your hand and arm may move at the wrong times and in the wrong order so that your hand shakes uncontrollably or even twists, spilling the water.

Brain Cells

The true mystery of the brain lies at a much more universal level than these regions: the individual nerve cells. It is among these cells that many scientists feel the real secrets of the brain reside. Dr. Jeffery Barker points out that "We don't yet know how these individual cells of the brain function when they talk to each other or, even, when they are in isolation, not at least the way we know how liver or white blood cells function. So, in our research, we are asking how the nervous system works by examining the functions of individual cells."

But what is known about the cells of the brain? All brains are composed of at least two types of cells, nerve cells, called *neurons,* and *glial* or *glia cells* (glia meaning "glue"). Until comparatively recently neurobiologists considered only neurons as important to the functioning of the brain. However, the glial cells are now thought to be of more importance than merely holding the neurons together. Indeed, since over a hundred billion glial cells make up the human brain, as compared to ten billion nerve cells, we might wonder at the waste of relegating so many cells to doing nothing but support neurons.

The glial cells help in the feeding of neurons. Most cells in the human body are able to pick up nutrition directly from the circulating blood. They also pick up everything else floating in the blood, some of which can kill the cell. For most cells this doesn't matter as long as not too many die at once since their fellows will quickly reproduce new ones. Indeed, the cells in the entire human body are replaced every ninety days. Nerve cells, however, are not able to reproduce. After childhood, the neurons lose this ability and never regain it. Thus, when a neuron dies, it is not replaced. The glial cells, therefore, act as a filter to keep harmful substances out of the nerve cells. They can be viewed as the final line of defense for the brain, supernannies looking after their delicate charges.

An additional role for the glial cells, and one still being investigated, is in memory. They also appear to be part of a communication system in the brain that is quite separate from that of neurons. Further, according to Dr. Richard Restak, these cells may be capable of starting and ending seizures.

Even with this increased interest in glial cells, neurons are still considered the functioning core for both the brain and the entire nervous system. These cells are not scattered uniformly throughout the brain, but are found in clumps and groups that correspond to active areas in the brain such as the motor and sensory cortexes of the cerebrum. Thus, watching your favorite TV show stimulates the neurons in the visual cortex and in the pleasure center within your hypothalamus. Standing up and reaching for a book set off the nerve cells in your brain stem and cerebellum.

Like the interior of any other cell in the body, the neuron has a nucleus and cytoplasm. Unlike other cells, the neuron has, emerging from its body, several branching tendrils called *dendrites,* appropriately derived from the Greek word for tree (see Figure 9). Also, extending from the nerve cell is a long fiber called an *axon,* meaning "axis." This is unbranched for most of its length. Through its dendrites, the nerve cell receives impulses from other nerve cells. It then passes these impulses along its axon to the next neuron. Because of the multiple branching of the dendrites, the neuron may receive signals from hundreds, perhaps thousands of other neurons, although not at the same time. Out of this large number of connections arises the complexity of the human brain.

Neurons oddly enough have no contact with one another. Al-

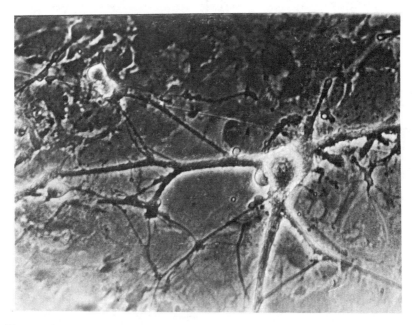

Neuron from a mouse's spinal column. Emerging from the cell body are the branched dendrites and the long axon. (Courtesy Jeffery Barker, National Institute of Neurological and Communicative Disorders and Stroke)

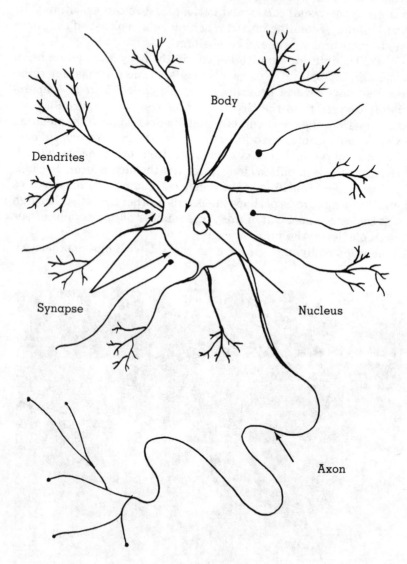

Figure 9. Neuron or nerve cell.

though they conduct an electrical impulse, neurons are not the equivalent of a biological copper wire. Instead, between each dendrite and each axon is a small gap. This gap is called the *synapse,* which in Greek, ironically means "union," the one thing it is not. The number of synapses between neurons tells us how many possible routes there are in the brain. According to Dr. David Hubel, Nobel Prize Laureate, this number may be as high as one hundred trillion in the human brain.

The axon of the neuron is surrounded by a fatty layer called the *myelin sheath,* myelin meaning "marrow." This sheath has periodic gaps so that it looks like a string of long, cyclindrical beads. It seems to serve two purposes. First, it insulates the axon from other cells so that it does not lose the electrical charge that accompanies nerve transmission. Second, it increases the speed of nerve transmission. A nerve fiber without a myelin sheath has a slower signal than one of the same size with such a sheath. A nerve impulse travels the entire length of a six-foot adult human being in two-tenths of a second or twenty miles an hour.

Within the neuron, a nerve signal is generally transmitted electrically. Such signals or impulses are generated through the movement of positively charged sodium and potassium ions (see Figure 10). Ions either have a positive or negative electrical charge and are created from atoms, which have no charge at all. An atom has a zero charge because it has an equal number of negatively charged particles, called *electrons,* and positively charged particles, called *protons.* An atom becomes a positive ion when it loses an electron, thus giving it one more proton than the number of electrons. It becomes a negative ion when it picks up an extra electron, giving it one more electron than the number of protons.

The sodium and potassium ions involved with the neuron have lost one electron each, and each has a positive electrical charge of one. Since both have lost only one electron, they are electrically equal. When a nerve cell is at rest, not transmitting a signal, the sodium ions are outside the cell wall or membrane and the potassium ions are inside. The membrane pushes any sodium ions that get into the cell out.

A neuron becomes active when it receives, through one of its dendrites, a signal from another nerve cell. The whole nervous system resembles a gigantic bucket brigade. Signals are passed from neuron to neuron much like the buckets are passed from person to person. When the neuron is activated, its membrane starts allowing sodium ions to enter the cell. The entrance of the sodium ions forces the

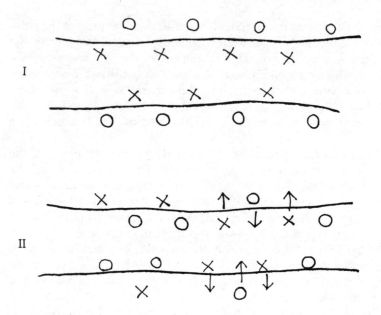

Figure 10. Positioning of sodium ions (Na$^+$) and potassium ions (K$^+$) in neuron at rest (I) and neuron in action (II).

potassium ions out. Since both ions have the same charge, they repel each other. You can see the same principle if you try to join the north poles of two magnets together. As you bring them closer together, you can feel them pushing harder and harder against one another. In the same way, the sodium ions push the potassium ions out.

The sodium ions are smaller, and they move more quickly into the cell than the potassium ions can move out. The neuron consequently takes on a slightly positive charge. At rest, the nerve cell is 70 millivolts less than its exterior. (A millivolt is equal to a thousandth of a volt. Standard house current is 120 millivolts, so you can see how small the electrical charge we are talking about is.) During the time the sodium ions are moving into the nerve cell, the neuron's interior reaches a maximum voltage of 120 volts. The cell is now 50 millivolts higher than its exterior, and this difference creates an electrical current, the nerve signal.

The neuron's membrane only becomes porous to the sodium ions a section at a time. The first section is activated by the initial reception of the signal at the dendrite. When this part of the cell reaches its 120-millivolt peak, it then activates the next portion of the neuron's membrane. And so the process continues until the signal is passed to the nerve cell's axon. Here it is sent across the synapse to the next neuron.

Eventually, the potassium and sodium ions are in equal numbers inside and outside the neuron. The charge of the neuron's interior is now the same as its exterior, and the nerve transmission stops. Before the nerve cell can operate again, the sodium ions must be pumped back outside the cell. This allows the potassium to reenter. Until this pumping process is complete, the neuron can do nothing. Yet even with this necessary recovery period, nerve cells can transmit between 250 and 2,500 impulses per second.

But how does the nerve impulse cross the synapse, that gap lying between each neuron? At one time, researchers thought that the signal jumped this space, punching its way across the synapse. The signal, however, doesn't have the strength for such a leap. If it did try to jump the synapse, it would fall short like a man trying to leap across too wide a chasm.

The answer lies with the chemical *acetylcholine*. The components for this chemical, of which one is acetic acid, which gives vinegar its distinctive smell, are found in all nerve cells. When the nerve impulse reaches the axon, it stimulates the formation of acetylcholine. This substance can easily flow across the synapse and activate the next neuron (see Figure 11). Acetylcholine is also involved with allowing sodium ions to enter the neuron. When it hits the dendrite of the next

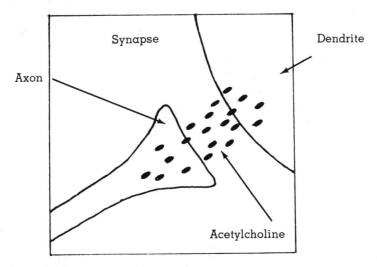

Figure 11. Acetylcholine moving from axon of one neuron to dendrite of a second neuron.

cell, that cell begins manufacturing more acetylcholine. This in turn opens each section of the neuron's membrane to the sodium ions.

The process, however, is not yet complete. Acetylcholine can't just be left to float around on its own. If it did, the sodium ions would remain in the cell, and nerve transmission would end. So, we have another chemical, *cholinesterase,* which breaks up acetylcholine so that it can do no mischief once its job is done. This acetylcholine-cholinesterase cycle is quite rapid, easily keeping pace with the speed of nerve transmission. Without cholinesterase, acetylcholine is not broken down, and, if acetylcholine remains intact, it prevents the exclusion of sodium ions from the inside of the neuron. All of which means that nerve transmission ceases. When the neurons stop working, the heart stops beating because the heart functions only as long as its muscles are stimulated by signals along the vagus nerve. Any lengthy interference, therefore, in the manufacture of cholinesterase causes death.

Several natural inhibitors of cholinesterase exist. The most famous of these is curare, used by South American Indians to poison arrowheads, and a popular poison in numerous 1930's and 1940's mysteries and movie serials. Many nerve gases are also cholinesterase inhibitors. The first of these were manufactured by the Germans during World War II, but the Germans refrained from making use of them. Since then both the United States and the Soviet Union have developed and stockpiled laboratory-created cholinesterases. Cholinesterase inhibitors, however, need not be used merely as weapons. Some people suffer from insufficient production of acetylcholine, particularly where nerves join the muscles of arms and legs. For these people, a slowdown in the creation of cholinesterase means that their muscles can receive the necessary stimulus to act, and so small doses of cholinesterase inhibitors, dangerous to most of us, are a medication for them.

The Mysterious Brain

Although no one claims to understand fully the operation of the neuron, neurobiologists have recognized for years that at least the dendrite-axon process is basically an "on/off" switch. Thus, at least in part, neurons act according to the "all-or-none law." A neuron either transmits its signal at full strength, or it does nothing. A weak signal

DID THE DOGS DO IT?

One of the most serious of neurological diseases is multiple sclerosis (MS), whose victims normally contract it between the ages of 17 and 40. A major problem in diagnosing this disorder is the confusion of symptoms. Although MS breaks down the myelin sheath, the fatty layer, of the neuron, it also produces a wide variety of effects. An MS sufferer may slowly lose feeling in one side of his or her body, or may have problems seeing or speaking. Complete paralysis is not unknown, although it is not inevitable. In addition, some victims may suddenly lose most of these symptoms—sometimes permanently, sometimes not.

The cause of MS has been elusive. The disease is neither contagious nor hereditary. No consistent pattern that fitted conventional diseases worked for MS. In 1957, Dr. Carleton Gajdusek began studying *Kuru*, a degenerative nerve disorder found among New Guinea tribesmen who honored their dead by eating them, including those who had died from *Kuru*. Gajdusek, at first, thought that the infection was transmitted through eating the diseased tissue of the *Kuru* victim's brain. However, he could see no illness developing in those who had done the eating, and when he injected a monkey with *Kuru* tissue extract, he found that nothing happened. At least, not immediately. After several months, the injected monkey developed *Kuru* and died a few months later. Gajdusek postulated that this disease was caused by what he called a slow virus. Such slow viruses, instead of immediately attacking their host's system, would wait months, perhaps years, before suddenly becoming active and deadly.

Multiple sclerosis would seem to be caused by such a slow virus. The victims would be infected and then years later, maybe even thousands of miles away, would come down with MS. The evidence points to dogs as the infecting agents. However, we have nothing to fear from healthy dogs, only from those suffering from canine distemper, a degenerative nerve disease in dogs that is similar to MS. Most communities in this country and in other western countries require that puppies be inoculated against canine distemper. What is the evidence for this link between MS and canine distemper? In one household when the family dog came down with canine distemper, three out of four sisters developed MS; the fourth sister was away from home at this time. The Faore Islands, between Iceland and Greenland, had never reported a case of MS prior to 1943. Between 1943 and 1960, a small epidemic of multiple sclerosis swept the islands. In the 1940's, British troops were stationed in these islands, and the officers brought their dogs. A wave of canine distemper swept the islands and was soon followed by the first cases of MS. Since 1957, canine distemper has disappeared from the Faore Islands. So has MS.

Will this knowledge that multiple sclerosis is caused by a slow virus, possibly related to canine distemper, hasten a cure for MS? Only time will tell. And what other slow virus diseases exist and how common are they? Again, time will tell.

---

will not activate a neuron. Increasingly stronger signals will only result in the neuron sending its impulses at full strength. A stronger signal cannot produce a stronger response.

Here, we have only begun to scratch the surface of the workings of the brain, and, already, we see just how complicated and complex it is. Obviously such complexity gives researchers difficulty, yet it also presents them with a constant variety of challenges and problems to investigate. Never think for a moment that, even today, the brain is easy to study. It has taken a long time for us to reach the understanding of the brain that we now have, and, in the next chapter, we shall see what some of the tools are that helped and are still helping to create that understanding.

2

Breaching the Fortress: Discovering the Brain

Ask Dr. John Eric Holmes of the University of Southern California about the essential difference between brain research in the 1980's and the 1950's, and he says, "The obvious difference is technology. That's how research gets done. So much of research is 'gee, now that we've got this gadget, what can we do with it?'" Indeed, much of the course of neurobiology has been set through the development of one instrument or technique after another. Although what Dr. Holmes says is true of all science, it is particularly true of brain research. The brain is so well-protected that it has been a major problem just getting at it without killing the brain in the process. Certainly investigating the brain has called for a great deal of ingenuity and, perhaps of even more importance, patience and persistence.

We can't fully appreciate what is being learned about the brain and how this knowledge is being gained without some background about what scientists did in the past and how they did it. The first question was not "What does the brain do?" or "How does it do it?" but "Where do we start?" The brain, you might say, but, when you know little about the human body, the brain isn't necessarily the first choice. Indeed, many earlier cultures such as the Hindus, Hebrews, and Chinese did not start with the brain because they felt it was an inferior organ. For them the heart was the center of intelligence, consciousness, and emotion. The Egyptians of the same period were so contemptuous of the brain that, when embalming a body, they extracted the brain piece by piece through the nose and threw it away. They carefully retained the heart and liver, which they thought performed the brain's functions.

The brain found its first "champions" in the Greeks. Plato was convinced that the brain was the seat of consciousness because it was spherical in shape. For Plato, the sphere represented perfection. But not all Greeks were ready to shift their loyalty to the brain. Many preferred the dynamic action of the heart to the quiescent brain. No less a person than Aristotle sneered at the notion that the brain was important for sensation. When he touched the brain of a living animal, he saw no reaction. Times were changing, however. In the second century A.D., the Greek physician Galen repeated Aristotle's experiment, but he came to the opposite conclusion. Galen did not just touch the brain of a living animal, but pressed it. He noted that the animal lost all sensation and voluntary movement. He then squeezed the heart, and the animal squirmed showing no loss of sensation or movement. Galen felt that, since only pressure on the brain affected sensation and movement, the brain must logically control these functions. The brain then became the object of subsequent research. Knowledge about the brain, however, was not soon in coming. The tools and techniques were still several centuries in the future. Until the Renaissance in the fourteenth century, the brain remained as unknown as the North American continent to most of medieval Europe.

Tools and Techniques

According to Dr. David Hubel, the three most essential tools neurologists had for studying the brain were "the microscope, the microelectrode, and stains that selectively mark neural tissue." To these can be added the *electroencephalogram (EEG),* the *computerized axial tomography (CAT) scanner,* and the *positron emission transaxial tomography (PETT) scanner.* All of these latter instruments allow scientists to examine the brain and its operations without opening the skull. In many ways, the EEG and the CAT and PETT scanners are the telescopes of the brain researcher, and the microelectrodes and the stains are the planetary probes. In the study of the brain, however, the "telescopes" may tell us more about the brain than the physical probes. They certainly are less disruptive and destructive.

Indeed, damage and destruction were key elements in our coming to understand much of the brain's function. Early researchers discovered which areas of the brain governed which parts of the body and which senses by dissecting the brains of people who suffered from every type of brain disorder from epilepsy to cerebral palsy. Paul Broca in the nineteenth century found one of the centers controlling speech by examining, after death, the brains of those with speech problems. Scientists commonly would injure or destroy different areas in the brains of dogs or cats. Then they would watch to see what the damage caused. Even much of the knowledge we have about the relationship between personality, behavior, and the brain was obtained by observing people and animals with brain injuries. In 1848, a construction foreman, Phineas Gage, had a metal rod blasted up through his left cheek and out the right side of his skull. Miraculously he lived, but he wasn't the same Phineas Gage. Physically he showed no effects from the accident, but whereas before Gage had been a hardworking, quiet man, he now was loud, abusive, and without purpose. Such case histories filled the annals of psychology for years. Dependency on brain damage for research was not eliminated until the invention of the *microelectrode*. This allowed investigators not only to look at the brain in more subtle and less destructive ways, but also to look at normal, healthy brains.

The Microscope

The microscope was the first great invention to be of use in neurological research. In the middle 1600's, Anton van Leeuwenhoek constructed the first simple microscope, which, like the telescope before it, opened up whole new worlds. Van Leeuwenhoek's microscope was not very powerful, and, a few years later, Robert Hooke, a contemporary and sometimes rival of Sir Isaac Newton, developed the compound microscope. Hooke's microscope had three lenses, two of which were mounted in a movable tube. The third was fixed in place just above the microscope's stage, on which the slide-mounted specimen was placed for observation. By moving the tube containing the first two lenses, Hooke could greatly increase or decrease the magnification and was able to see a larger variety of objects than van Leeuwenhoek with his simple microscope.

Hooke and his contemporaries were quick to put slices of brain and neural tissue under this new microscope. Unfortunately, these early models had problems with the lens system, and the researchers were not always certain about what they saw. In fact, few saw quite the same thing. Thus van Leeuwenhoek saw nerve fibers as a string of globules; a century later, Martin Ledermüller viewed them as collections of hollow tubes. The lens problem with the compound microscope was solved in the nineteenth century by M. Selligue. With this improvement, researchers were no longer bothered by optical discrepancies and distortion. Indeed, by 1837, the Czech Jan Purkinje, using Selligue's new microscope, was able to describe accurately the general physical characteristics of nerve cells.

Although the compound microscope is still used frequently today, it has been supplanted by the electron microscope when more detail is required. The electron microscope employs a shaped magnetic field that focuses on electron beam. According to the 1924 de Broglie theory, an electron has many of the same properties as light and can and does form an image, the basis of the electron microscope.

Assuming that what we can see with our naked eyes is zero, then the simple microscope can magnify things 600 times. With it, we can see some microorganisms such as the amoeba and the larger details of tissues. The compound microscope extends our field of vision even more since it magnifies things 6,000 times. With it, we can see bacteria and the cells that make up body tissue. Finally, the electron microscope has a magnification of 600,000, which not only lets us see such extraordinarily small objects as viruses, but even some of the larger molecules that go into making up the cells of our bodies such as nerve cells.

Let's return to the nineteenth century for a moment, however. The lens problem with the compound microscope was solved, but a second problem remained. Neurons, in fact all neural tissue, are transparent to both light and electrons. Therefore, direct observation of nerve cells is frustrating since it is difficult to see more than the most obvious details. Researchers were unable even to decide whether neurons were physically connected or separated from every other cell. As we now know, neurons are separated, but, in the nineteenth century, because of the difficulty in tracing the full length of a nerve cell and because scientists could not see how divided cells could transmit nerve impulses, a substantial number of researchers favored the connected neuron theory. To them, the neural network was just like a city's water system with nerve impulses flowing through the neurons like water through pipes. The neatness of the theory was definitely attractive, but wrong.

Stains

The answer was found using *stains*. Stains are any chemicals that, when applied to tissues, color different parts of the tissue in varying degrees. Thus the stain provides enough contrast to see the part being studied. Such contrast is particularly important in the study of neurons, whose long axon and many-branched dendrites make it difficult to see in isolation from the surrounding material. If you had a patterned rug whose fibers were all white, you would find it difficult to see the patterns. But, by dyeing the fibers composing the patterns, say red, you could easily not only see the patterns clearly, but also see and measure their extent. The process is much the same with biological stains.

The first stain of importance to neural research was carmine and allowed researchers to map out the outline of neurons. It did not, however, answer the major question whether or not neurons were connected. In 1875, an Italian anatomist Camillo Golgi developed a stain that would eventually yield an answer. The stain, appropriately known as *Golgi stain* or the *Golgi Method,* has provided, according to neurobiologists such as David Hubel and Valentine Braitenberg, more information about the neural structure of the brain than all the other pre-1970 methods combined.

The Golgi Method has its problems, however. It takes a week of soaking the tissue in several solutions. The most important is silver nitrate (one of the elements in photographic film). Despite this tedious process, the results are excellent. The Golgi stain only colors scattered, single neurons. The nerve cell, now reddish-black, stands out from the unstained background. Even today, no one knows why this stain only marks a single neuron. Such a mystery has not, however, diminished the usefulness of the Golgi Method. Still, even

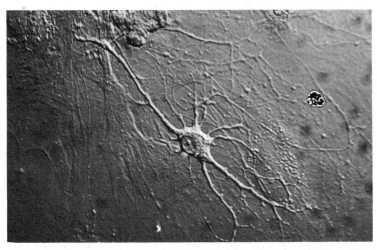

Stained neuron from a mouse's spinal column. (Courtesy Jeffery Barker, National Institute of Neurological and Communicative Disorders and Stroke)

with one of the most remarkable research tools ever developed, neurologists were not able to establish how one neuron fed into another. The Golgi Method is almost more an art than a science. The preparation is not only tedious, but fairly difficult, particularly for the early researchers who had no way of knowing what strength their solutions should be for the best results. In fact, the initial frustration with the use of this stain was so great that even Golgi, the inventor of the process, gave up in disgust.

If Golgi retreated from his own method, Santiago Ramón y Cajal, a Spanish biologist, did not, and in 1889 Cajal demonstrated his refined techniques using the Golgi stain. Not only did he establish through his research that neurons are separate from one another, but he developed the procedures for the use of the Golgi stain that are still being employed today.

Naturally, the Golgi stain is not the only chemical that has proven useful in the study of the brain. The Nissl stain colors the neurons' nuclei, the central portion of any cell. Scientists can then count the number of nerve cells in a tissue sample, giving them some idea of the number of nerve cells in the brain itself. Other silver-based chemicals are used to examine nerve fibers.

Electrically Stimulating the Brain

The development of the microscope combined with various staining techniques taught neurobiologists a great deal about the structure of the brain, particularly the nerve cell. Neither, however, helped much in learning about how the brain operated. Various experiments in the eighteenth century established that nerve impulses were electrical in nature. Through the middle of the nineteenth century, many experimenters stimulated the muscles of various animals. Most notable was Luigi Galvani, who worked with dissected frog legs. His principles of galvanism were so famous that they were used by such writers as Mary Shelley in her novel *Frankenstein* and Edgar Allan Poe in several of his short stories.

If electricity could affect the muscles, what could it do to the brain itself? So the next step was to stimulate areas of the brain directly and see what happened. Two Berlin doctors, Gustav Fritsch and Eduard Hitzig, were among the first to do so. Hitzig had already done some work on his own before teaming up with Fritsch as head doctor at a military hospital. He applied wires running from a battery to the surface of the brains of soldiers who had part of their skulls shot away while fighting, achieving for Hitzig something of a ghoulish reputation. He and Fritsch continued these experiments using live dogs. They would open the skulls and electrically stimulate different areas, noting whether the dog moved its right front leg, lifted its tail, or whether nothing happened. In this way, they began mapping the motor area. Since they did not have a laboratory, they performed these experiments on Mrs. Hitzig's dressing table. What her reaction was, history does not record.

Hitzig and Fritsch were the first researchers to use electrodes to stimulate directly a living brain. They were soon followed by many others, most of whom were interested in stimulating more than just the surface of the brain. In 1874, an American doctor, Roberts Bartholow, inserted an electrode into the brain of Mary Rafferty, who had a cancer of the scalp that had eaten a hole in her skull. It was through this hole that Bartholow inserted his electrode. Like Hitzig, Bartholow's reputation suffered, and he had to find a new home after Mary Rafferty's death, which was not related to these experiments. The electrode, however, survived, and it is still being used today.

Although electrodes allow scientists to see how large areas of the brain function, they do not allow researchers to look at single nerve cells. They are just too big. The technology of the 1930's, however, had the answer, the microelectrode, Hubel's third essential tool of the neurobiologist (see Figure 1). It takes a microscope to see a neuron. It takes one to see the tip of a microelectrode too. Since the tip is tinier than the smallest nerve cell, it can be slipped into any size brain cell.

No one believes that every neuron can be checked using the microelectrode. "It would take several thousand years," guesses Dr. Michael Phelps. Yet, cells of specific interest can be checked. In Chapter 4, we will look at Hubel and Wiesel's use of the microelectrode to trace vision from the eye to the visual cortex. In all uses of the microelectrode, the researcher inserts the microelectrode, then manipulates the target cell to fire. The firing produces a current that runs up the microelectrode to recording instruments. In many cases, the microelectrode can insert a stain into the neuron being monitored. Later, in animal experiments, the brain can be dissected, and the scientists can tell exactly which cell they were recording since it will stand out because of the injected stain.

No matter how enthusiastic we are about scientific and technological research, we are often plagued by suspicions and doubts

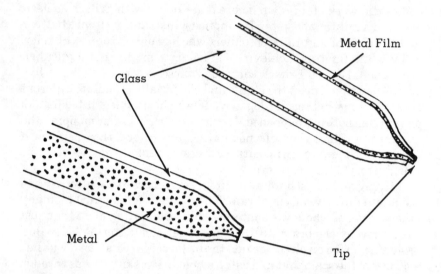

Figure 1.   Two types of microelectrodes.

that such research may cause more harm than good. Unfortunately, our present world gives us reason for these fears. Nuclear research may have given us new treatments for cancer, but it has also given us the nuclear bomb. DNA recombinant research is giving us new tools, but it could also give us new biological weapons. Brain research has not escaped these fears. The dark side of such study is haunted by the specter of control. If we learn enough about the brain and its operations not only to understand it, but also to eliminate both mental and physical disorders, we may possibly be giving the unscrupulous among us a weapon with which to control us.

In the 1950's, the sophisticated studies using electrodes gave rise to this fear. During this period, electrodes were placed in the pleasure center, the hypothalamus, of rats. The rat could be pleasurably stimulated when a current ran through the electrode. When rats were allowed to choose between pushing a button that would give them food or pushing a button that activated the electrode and the pleasure center, they pushed the electrode button. They would pick this button over not only food, but also sleep and sex. Many people became afraid that human beings would also choose the electronically activated pleasure center just like the rats. Many saw civilization ending in a fury of self-indulgence. The main fear was that a ruthless group could gain control of those having such implanted electrodes, and, by denying these electrode-wearers pleasure, this group would have total

PHRENOLOGY: A WRONG ROAD

In the twentieth century, studying the brain without opening the skull and physically invading the brain itself has become possible with various electronic tools. Earlier scientists also wanted to study the brain without having to go through the thick bone of the skull. One method they used was phrenology.

At the beginning of the nineteenth century, Franz Joseph Gall, an Austrian doctor, put forward the theory that the surface of the brain was divided into areas. Each of these areas controlled a different function from moving the arm to determining intelligence. Gall was not too far off what was later to be accepted as fact, the specialization of regions of the brain. Later researchers, however, would decide that such regions went deep into the brain rather than merely lying along the brain's surface.

Gall, however, went on to make another assumption that was not correct. He was convinced that the various areas of the brain's surface were of different sizes according to how much use they received and that this variation in size was reflected by bumps and indentations in the skull. Thus, by feeling a person's skull and knowing what regions lay underneath, Gall was certain he could tell what parts of that person's brain were most active. Gall decided, for example, that people with good memories had protruding eyes since, for him, memory was located in that part of the brain just behind the eyes.

Phrenology caught on rapidly, and Gall's followers were quick to expand upon his theories. At phrenology's height, such people as J.W. Redfield, a New York physician, and L.N. Fowler were claiming to have located 160 centers of brain ability through the examination of the skull's contours. Fowler in 1916 marketed a bust which charted 100 of these regions. All systems of phrenology claimed to be able to account for everything from love to economy to patriotism to criminal behavior.

Unfortunately for phrenology, no clear-cut connection between brain size and ability has ever been discovered. Lord Byron, the famous nineteenth-century British poet, had a brain weighing over six pounds, while the nineteenth-century American poet Walt Whitman had one weighing slightly under four pounds. Both have been considered literary geniuses. Also, no correlation exists between the contour of the skull's outer surface and the surface of the brain.

Ironically, phrenology did lead neurologists into at least one right pathway. From its insistence on the specialization of regions of the brain, researchers began examining with electrodes to see what exactly happened when various parts of the brain were stimulated. Today's division of the brain owes much to this nineteenth-century fad, phrenology.

---

command. Still others felt that the process could be simpler than that. Why not just put electrodes into those parts of the brain that would insure obedience when the electrode was activated?

A quarter of a century later, these fears have disappeared. Electrodes are not particularly convenient, and the drilling of holes in the skull for the electrode mounts, although not painful, is certainly not attractive to the average person. Nor is the process cheap. Expense and unpleasantness insure that electronic pleasure addiction is unlikely. Furthermore, governmental control of a population through the use of electrodes is impractical. Indeed, at the moment, brain research is not a threat to us or our society. As David Hubel says, "I don't think anyone is going to be able to do great harm from what's found in brain research for a long, long time. We don't know enough." We should remember too that ignorance is not safety. Ignorance of simple sanitation has killed more people than all wars combined.

The electrode and the microelectrode have provided the majority of our information about the functioning of the living brain. Unfortunately, in placing an electrode in the brain, scientists are also placing a foreign object in the brain as well, thus "contaminating" it. Although neither electrodes nor microelectrodes appear to do any damage—indeed patients undergoing constant monitoring often have them in place for days or weeks at a time without adverse effect—they may, in some subtle fashion, affect the results they obtain. Science has always had to cope with several persistent problems, but one of the most annoying is the possible effect observation has on the object being studied. We have all seen films in which one side of an ant colony has been replaced by glass so that the ants' activity can be photographed and studied. But how do we know that ants act the same way in a normally dirt-enclosed, underground nest? We don't; however, if the glass-walled setup is made as close to the ants' normal environment as possible, we can feel reassured about what we are seeing. And, of course, we can gather other data about ant behavior from other types of observation and see how this information matches with what we see through the glass.

Brain researchers have the same problem. Does the electrode change the way the brain works? As far as anyone can tell, no, but, obviously, the best way to be sure about the validity of brain observation is to learn to examine the brain's operation from outside the skull. We may still have to worry about our methods of study interfering with the functions being examined, but at least we will be dealing with a brain free of invading probes and instruments. We are then one step closer to the actual brain itself.

The EEG

The 1970's has seen an increase in non-invasive techniques, techniques not requiring physical entry into the brain. One of the oldest non-invasive instruments, the electroencephalogram (the EEG), was developed some fifty years ago. The principle on which the EEG operates, the ability to detect brain activity through electrodes placed on the skull, was first formulated over a century ago by a British physician, Richard Caton.

The 1920's in Germany was a turbulent and often chaotic period, from which we would expect little in the way of progress. Yet, during these years, Hans Berger began experimenting with the placement of electrodes on the scalp. Although he suffered through a number of unsuccessful experiments, he was the first researcher to record brain waves, which eventually led to the creation of the EEG.

What exactly was Berger and later EEG-users measuring? What are called brain waves are changes in *electric potential* in the brain. Electric potential is merely the separation of negative and positive charges. As we saw in Chapter 1, the neuron at rest has such a separation of charge, giving its interior a negative charge in relation to its exterior. When activated, the neuron still has an electric potential as its interior briefly becomes more positive than its exterior.

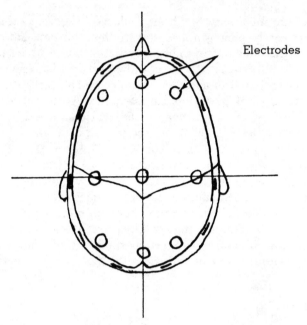

Figure 2.   Possible placement of EEG electrodes on scalp.

Thus, fluctuations in electric potential, separation of negative and positive charges, in the brain are not surprising.

A dozen or so electrodes, depending on the machine being used, are pasted to a subject's scalp (see Figure 2). Originally, each electrode was connected to its own recorder. A long strip of paper rolls across the top of the recorder, not unlike a typewriter ribbon or a cassette tape feeding between the two holding spools. A pen is fixed so that it moves from the bottom of the paper to the top according to the input it gets from the electrode. If the brain wave disappears, the pen makes a straight line from right to left, bisecting the paper. When the EEG is activated, the pen draws a series of valleys and peaks, whose size depends upon the type of brain wave being measured (see Figure 3).

Obviously, even in a short run, a dozen electrodes would produce a large number of paper sheets with brain wave curves on them. A researcher who was trying to determine what effect, let us say, a flash of light had on various brain wave patterns would find himself only able to read one record at a time. Even with the paper marked in time intervals, this harried scientist would still have a dozen recording

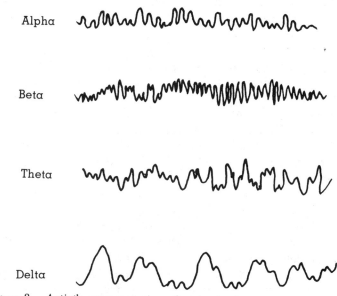

Alpha

Beta

Theta

Delta

Figure 3. Artist's representation of major brain waves.

strips to look at and to evaluate. No wonder EEG practitioners were considered more artists than scientists. With the advent of the computer, researchers were able to feed the information from the electrodes into a computer for analysis and comparison. The final readout was a composite of all the data recorded and was much easier to understand. Multi-channel magnetic tapes, some having as many as twenty-eight tracks (the average home recording tape has four tracks), made storage of this electrode information easier. Researchers could play all the data out at once or only a single track.

Even with an increase in technology, the problems in actually taking EEG readings remained. Subjects are recorded generally lying down because, otherwise, movements of the arms, legs, or body can interfere with the recordings. Still, researchers have to contend with movement of scalp and facial muscles that give misleading EEG readings. A further complication arises when EEG operators attempt to determine what is and is not a normal brain wave pattern for any individual.

For years the EEG was most valuable as a diagnostic, rather than an investigative, machine. Because brain waves are as unique as the individual to which they belong, it is sometimes difficult to make a quick, accurate diagnosis. For example, although a *grand mal*

seizure makes a dramatic recording, as seen in Figure 4, some
people's EEGs indicate disorders such as epilepsy, although they
show no actual signs of the problem. EEGs can even be superfluous,
as in the case again of epilepsy, the symptoms of which may be
obvious to the naked eye. Nevertheless, the EEG is useful. For instance, the symptoms of *petit mal* and other forms of epilepsy may
sometimes be confused with those of other disorders. Brain wave
patterns often show certain changes that can help determine whether
the doctor is or is not dealing with epilepsy. Additionally, until
recently, the EEG was used in discovering the presence and sometimes the placement of brain tumors. Such tumors affected the normal brain wave patterns, and a skilled EEG operator could see this in
the recordings obtained.

Berger identified two types of brain waves, *alpha* and *beta*. Since
then scientists have discovered many others. Of these, *theta* and *delta*
are considered the most important. Although alpha waves can occasionally be detected from most areas of the cerebrum, generally they
seem to be associated with the visual cortex. Berger, who at first
assumed alpha waves indicated conscious thought, was surprised
that they disappeared when the subject had to respond to the touch of
a glass rod or to a question. Only when the subject's eyes were closed,
did alpha waves appear; when the eyes were opened, they were gone.
They also disappeared when the subject went to sleep. Alpha waves
indicate the readiness of the cerebrum to respond to outside stimuli.
When not active, the brain is like an idling motor, and the alpha

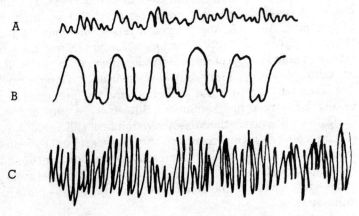

Figure 4. Artist's representation of normal alpha waves (A), alpha waves for
petit mal *epileptic seizure (B), and alpha waves for* grand mal *epileptic seizure*
(C).

waves signal this idling. Naturally, either action or sleep destroys the need for this ready state and the need for alpha wave formation.

Beta waves come in two kinds, beta I and beta II. They originate in either the frontal or parietal lobes of the cerebrum. Beta I, like alpha waves, are an idling signal. Beta II, however, appear during periods of intense mental activity.

Theta waves, like beta waves, originate from the parietal lobes. They also are centered in the temporal lobes and are strongest (much stronger than alpha waves) in children until the age of five. After the age of six, they diminish in strength. In adults, they become strong when something pleasurable is suddenly interrupted. Also they are often very strong in some people suffering from mental disorders, especially serious psychopathic behavior.

Finally, delta waves, because of their stretched out peaks and valleys, are the "slow" brain waves of the major four. Delta waves appear normally in children and in sleeping adults. Adults who display delta waves when awake are generally suffering from some brain damage or disorder, and thus the presence of such waves is one method of diagnosis. Some connection may exist, as well, between delta waves and mental problems. One of the early EEG researchers, W. Grey Walter, felt that delta waves were a safety measure. According to him, when neurons in the brain are in danger from damage, disease, or fatigue, then the brain shuts down until the problem can be corrected, and the delta waves appear.

Recently a new brain wave, N400, has been detected. When an EEG subject is shown a nonsense sentence, such as, "The book walked away," the brain does a double take, and the N400 appears. N400 is equivalent to the brain saying "What?" or "Huh?" In the future, people who have reading problems can be hooked up to an EEG, and when they reach a passage or a sentence they cannot understand, the appearance of the N400 brain wave will alert therapists, and so doctors will know exactly where the problems in comprehension actually lie.

Earlier we said that brain waves are the measure of changes in electrical potential. But, changes in the electrical potential of what? This is a question that has never been satisfactorily answered and is one of the major problems in EEG research. At first, scientists such as Berger and Walter thought that the brain wave patterns reflected the firing of neurons in various regions of the brain. As we saw in the last chapter, when a nerve cell receives an impulse at its axon, it either responds to that impulse or it does not. This all-or-nothing response gives a very sharp, little spike if recorded, not at all like the smoother,

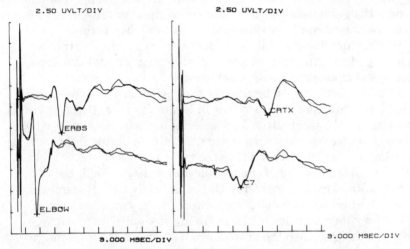

```
NAME :
AGE :        27
SEX : F                                        MN SEP
ID # :  592196                                          A LAT              D LAT
CASE # :         36
DIAGNOSIS : NORMAL                              ELBOW      4.140  ER-EL     5.160
PROCEDURE : MEDIAN NERVE SEP
DATE :  1/ 9/81                                 ERBS       9.300  C7-ER     3.120
REMARKS : MEDIAN NERVE SHORT LATENCY
SOMATOSENSORY EVOKED POTENTIALS WERE           C7        12.420  CX-C7     5.520
RECORDED.    ALL PERIPHERIAL AND CENTRAL
CONDUCTION TIMES WERE NORMAL.                  CRTX      17.940  CX-ER     8.640
TAG ID : F/27/N
```

*Paper recording of brain wave response pattern from nerve stimulation.
Courtesy of Nicolet Biomedical Instruments.*

flatter curves of a brain wave. These early EEG operators decided
that the waves were actually made from hundreds, perhaps thousands of the little spike-like neuron signals—so many that the sharp-
ness of the neurons' signal blended together forming the brain wave
curves. Listen to a packed football stadium several blocks away. You
cannot, as you could if you were in the stands, pick up individual
voices. What you hear is a large, uniform noise that rises and falls
with the action of the game. In much the same way, scientists originally accounted for the nature of brain waves.

     Unfortunately, they were wrong. Measurements, using micro-
electrodes, of neuron firings in regions from which brain waves
were simultaneously being recorded revealed no correlation between
the activation of nerve cells and the appearance or disappearance of
brain waves. Indeed, the brain waves were there as often as not when
the neurons were not active, or rather when the axon and cell body of
the neuron were not active.

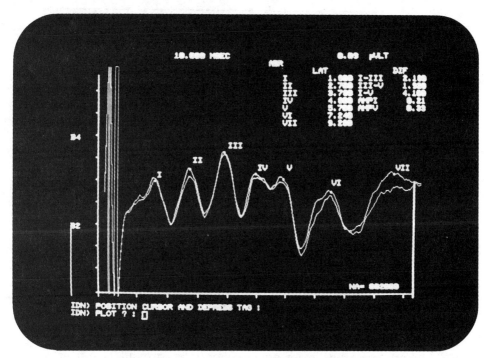

Brain wave response pattern from nerve stimulation as seen on the monitor screen of a Nicolet Pathfinder II evoked potential instrument. (Courtesy Nicolet Biomedical Instruments)

The massive network of the dendrites was another matter. The dendrite network does not operate quite so simply as do the axon and cell body of the nerve cell. Indeed, the all-or-nothing response of the nerve cell is not a feature of the dendrites. Single dendrite filaments are the same on/off switch that the cell body and axon are, but there are so many dendrites per neuron, and more than one receive signals at a time. So we have a fairly constant source of changing electrical potential. As Alan Gevins of EEG Systems Laboratory observes, "We're not picking up the all-or-nothing axonal potentials, but rather the graded postsynaptic dendritic potentials. They vary continuously." Remember our analogy of the football crowd. Instead of thinking of the crowd as a collection of individuals, think of it as a collection of groups made up of friends, clubs, bands, etc. Although at any one time, several people in each group may be quiet, others in the group will be talking, cheering, ordering drinks or food. So, no matter what a single person in the group may be doing, the group itself is constantly making some noise that goes into making the crowd sound.

JOHN L. KENNEDY AND THE CERAMIC SKULL

The EEG has been and continues to be a useful tool in brain research; however, despite a number of theories, the actual nature of brain waves is still unknown. Perhaps one of the oddest findings in the study of such waves was John L. Kennedy's paper in a 1959 issue of *Psychology Review*.

Kennedy made a rather simple model of the human skull and the brain. The skull was ceramic and filled with a gelatin substance the size and density of the human brain. Then, using a plunger to simulate the pulsing of blood vessels around the real brain, Kennedy attached electrodes to his ceramic skull. He got alpha waves. When Kennedy changed the rate of his plunger, he was able to record smaller waves. Later, he put a gum eraser into the gelatin mass and was able to locate it because of the slower waves coming from around the eraser. This is the way brain tumors are found using EEG's.

The results of Kennedy's experiment fit well with some earlier findings. He had noted that, of any group of normal people, some five percent had poor or nonexistent alpha waves. One man who showed no alpha waves had a small hole in the side of his skull from an accident. Kennedy could see the membranes surrounding the brain beating in time to the flow of blood through them.

Taking a small plastic plate, Kennedy placed it over the hole and bound it tight. When he checked the man with the EEG, he now recorded alpha waves. Removing the plate, Kennedy's recording again showed no alpha waves.

No one knows for sure what all this means. But brain waves may be mechanical in origin, not merely electrical.

Although the dendrite theory at least accounts for the smooth nature of the EEG brain waves, it still does not answer all the questions. According to one EEG specialist, "We still don't know how the brain creates these electrical signals. That's still a very fundamental question."

ALAN GEVINS

Alan Gevins is director of the EEG Systems Laboratory, one of the research centers working on developing the new generation of EEG equipment and programs.

Q: What basic improvements have you made in the EEG?
A: We are able to resolve smaller signals out of the background noise of the brain than was previously possible. We can see these signals through the use of advanced types of computerized signal processing.
Q: Is this due to a refinement of previous techniques?
A: No, the method itself is new. However, it does incorporate some steps from previous techniques.
Q: How does your method work?
A: There are about fifteen steps in it, and it uses just about every type of math known to man. To simplify. First, we need a very controlled experimental situation. To use an analogy, it makes no sense to apply an electron microscope to a contaminated or distorted specimen.

So, we have to have a very controlled experiment. That way everything you want to vary varies, and everything you don't want to vary doesn't. Thus, we have had people making two types of judgments: decoding a number or lining up an arrow with a target. We hold everything else constant, including the stimulus, the difficulty of the task, and the response.
Q: That eliminates as much interference as possible?
A: Yes. Next, we present the judgments to people in the form of a video game. We record a person's brain waves as they play the game. It takes about seven seconds per trial of the game, and we record several hundred trials from each person.

Then we average the brain waves synchronized with the appearance of the stimulus on the video screen over the several hundred trials. We get what is called an average evoked potential. This is the AEP, with peaks and valleys extending several hundred milliseconds after the stimulus.

We use the AEP to narrow down the time intervals to those in which something important is occurring. For the chosen intervals, we then measure the similarity of wave shapes from

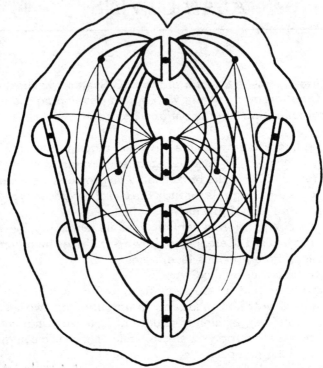

Figure 4a.

different areas of the brain to see how they line up.

We take measures of wave shape similarity and feed them into a mathematical pattern recognition program called SAM. SAM can recognize hidden patterns buried in vast quantities of data, patterns you can't see with your eyes.

SAM tells us how different areas of the brain line up in response to our experimental manipulations. We do this because the brain's electricity is so noisy that, without such pattern recognizers, we couldn't find the waves related to our video game.

Then we make line drawings to show which areas of the brain are related to which other areas during a very brief period of time (see Figure 4a).

Q: What have you learned about the functioning of the brain?

A: The first thing we learned is that the brain is complicated.

Even the simplest activity such as lining up an arrow with a target seems to involve interactions between all the areas of the brain we record. The interactions change very, very rapidly. They don't stay the same even for a tenth of a second.

Q: Then it's much more complex than the traditional models?

A: It's much more complicated, much more dynamic.

Q: Do you think this will make it more difficult to understand the brain's operation?

A: No, actually easier. Say you're looking at a distant city with a five power telescope. All you can see are maybe the tops of a couple of tall buildings.

Then someone comes along and builds a twenty power telescope. Now, you can see some smaller buildings and maybe start to see some of the details such as the shape of the windows.

Finally, someone builds a fifty power telescope. You can see people inside the offices. So, as the power of the instrument increases, you get more and more detail. Of course, you have to know where to point the telescope; you have to know what the important questions are.

But, without the more powerful telescope, you wouldn't have a chance.

Q: What do you think will come out of your research?

A: In the next five years, I would like to make a brain scanner based on the electricity of the human brain. This would allow us to look at several major "functional circuits" of the brain.

We could use the scanner on a patient with a brain injury, from a stroke or a car accident, to see how the functional circuits of his brain had been damaged, hand-eye coordination for example. A neurologist could use this information to choose the type of treatment which would best help the patient to recover.

The X Ray

The EEG was not the only non-invasive instrument in use during the early part of this century. Indeed, before it, there was the *X-ray* machine. We have all had our teeth X-rayed by a dentist and seen the black film with the ghostly outlines of our teeth that surround the

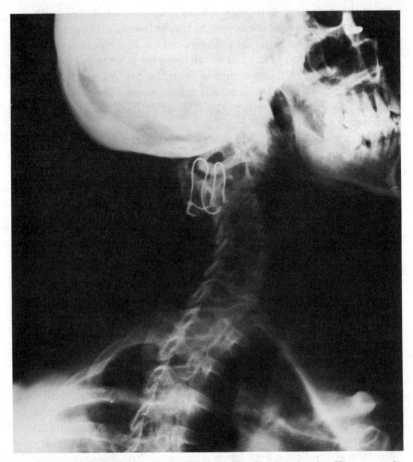

X ray of neck and skull. Notice how the skull absorbs the X rays so that, without the injection of some contrasting substance, the brain is hidden. The X ray is of a woman with arthritis; the wire at the top of the spine was implanted for strength. (Courtesy Nicolet Biomedical Instruments)

darker shadows of the roots. X-raying has been fairly common since the last quarter of the nineteenth century. X rays are similar to the visible light that our eyes can detect, but since these rays have a shorter wavelength, they are invisible to us. A metallic target is bombarded by a stream of electrons, producing the X rays, which are then shot through a patient to a square of photographic film (see Figure 5). The X rays are absorbed by different parts of the body at different rates; bones tend to absorb more X rays than do the softer tissues of the organs such as the lungs, heart, and brain. Thus, the X rays, passing through the patient's body, arrive at the photographic film having different intensities, depending on whether they had to pass through bone or soft tissue. These different intensities of the rays are represented on the film by images that vary in darkness and lightness. The image of bone is white, while that of organs is a dark gray, sometimes almost black. So the greater the absorption of X rays, the lighter the image.

Conventional X-raying has always provided limited access to the brain. The bone of the skull is so thick and so thoroughly surrounds the brain that it virtually wipes out the image of the brain. Methods were developed, however, to strengthen the contrast between the skull and the brain. Either a patient being examined for brain abnormalities had to be injected with air—a dangerous, lengthy, and painful process—or he had to be injected with a fluid that was opaque to X rays, also risky and uncomfortable since many of the dyes used were mildly poisonous. Even with such methods, the results were often far from satisfactory, and reading the X rays took training and skill. Also, with such dangerous and unpleasant techniques, X-raying was obviously restricted to the diagnosis of only serious brain disorders. To satisfy curiosity, researchers had to wait for a new machine.

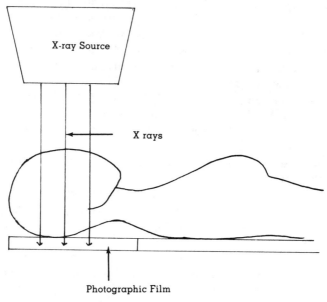

Figure 5. X-raying process.

The CAT Scanner

Such a machine was eventually produced and used for the first time in England in 1971. This was the computerized axial tomography scanner, better known as the CAT scanner. Its inventors, Allan Cormack and Godfrey Hounsfield, who won a Nobel Prize in 1979 for their creation, felt that the CAT scanner would open up the human body, and the brain in particular, to examination and study as the X-ray machine could never do.

They were right. Within eight years of that original machine's debut, 2,000 CAT scanners were in use throughout the world, certainly a mark of its popularity and usefulness. As John Eric Holmes says, "The amount of imaging we're getting now in the conventional CAT scanner is really fantastic. We're seeing anatomical structures we never even bothered to learn about before."

Although the CAT scanner uses X rays, it is a more precise instrument than the older X-ray machine. Why? "It has to do with the so-called tomographic principle where the X-ray tubes move about the patient's head and give information about a particular slice from many different positions," answers one CAT operator. "It is that information which is then computerized so that we end up with a better look at the soft tissue inside the skull. In conventional X-raying, the rays just pass through, and it takes fairly gross changes to show up." The CAT scanner has a large circular opening through which the patient or subject is moved back and forth along a slide. Mounted on a track in this circular opening are the X-ray tubes and the detectors. The X-ray tubes are contained in a unit called the gantry, and 180 degrees around the opening or directly opposite the gantry is the unit holding the X-ray detectors. Therefore, when the subject is slid into the scanner, he or she lies between the X-ray source and the pickups (see Figure 6).

When the machine is operating, the gantry, according to one doctor, "either rotates around or it slides back and forth, changing its angle each time, one or the other." The detector unit always remains opposite the X-ray source. When the sweep is completed, taking only two or three seconds in the latest GE scanners, a thin section of the patient's skull and brain has been penetrated by the X-ray beams. Just as with the conventional X-ray machine, when the X rays from the gantry pass through the patient's head, they are absorbed at different rates depending on the tissue through which they move. Emerging at different intensities, they strike the pickups, and the information is flashed to the computer.

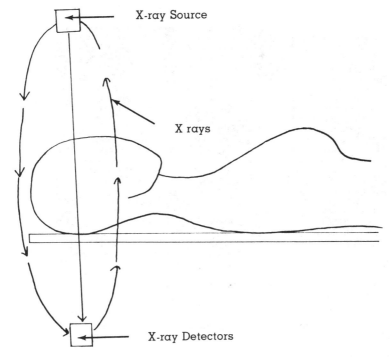

Figure 6. CAT scanning process.

The scanner operator then has the option of pulling the X-ray intensity values out of the computer as printed columns of figures or, more dramatically, of having the computer create an image on a computer display screen of the slice of the brain just scanned. This image can be photographed and studied in relation to the print-out figures. The photographed image is a *tomogram*, and the process of X-raying through a single plane of tissue is tomography. The tomogram shows all the details in the section of brain that has been scanned. Using a regular X-ray machine, you would have an image of the brain, but the structures closest to the skull and to the X-ray machine itself will obscure or even hide those farther into the brain. Of course, you could, using an X-ray machine, keep moving your subject around until you had X rayed the subject from all sides. In the process, however, you would have exposed the subject to a very large dosage of radiation. A single CAT-scanner sweep exposes the subject to only a quarter of the radiation from a traditional X-ray machine.

To comprehend fully the difference between tomogram and X ray, visualize a one-story house. A conventional X ray is like removing one wall of the house. You would be able to see the contents of the

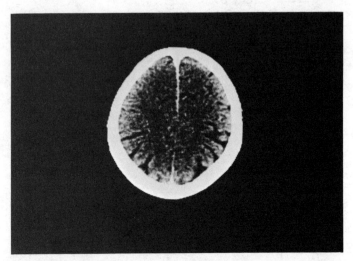

CAT scan of the cerebrum and cerebellum. White border is the skull and the lighter gray the cerebral and cerebellar cortexes. Same "view" as in the previous CAT scan. (Courtesy National Institute of Neurological and Communicative Disorders and Stroke)

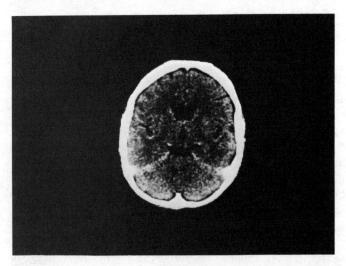

CAT scan showing both cerebral hemispheres. The white border is the skull and the lighter gray the cerebral cortex. Pretend you are looking down on someone's head; the bottom of the photo is the back of the head. (Courtesy National Institute of Neurological and Communicative Disorders and Stroke)

rooms on the other side of that wall. Beyond that, you might glimpse parts of the rest of the house through open doors, but you could not get a full picture of the other rooms and their contents. A CAT scan would, however, be like removing the roof. You could see down into the house and into every room. Now you could see those rooms that had formerly been hidden as well as their contents. For the first time in human history, we can look through the skull and directly at the brain as it is. We do not have to cut through the bone, or cut and section the brain with knives and scalpels. If the doctors and scientists look at the CAT scanner as a miracle machine, are they not justified?

The PETT Scanner

As useful as the CAT scanner is, it does have its limitations. You can make a tomogram using a CAT scanner of either a living or a dead brain. In both cases, you will get the same result: a reproduction of part of the brain's structure. But, using the positron emission transaxial tomography scanner, the PETT scanner, you can make a tomogram only of the living brain. With the dead brain, you get nothing. However, the PETT scanner is "showing us more than the structure of the body," says Dr. Michael Phelps of the Laboratory of Nuclear Medicine at UCLA (perhaps the leading positron tomography research center in the world). "Now the image with positron tomography not only will show us structure, but also will give us a map of body chemistry, not just the body structure." With this scanner, we can watch the brain as it works.

To understand the operation of the PETT scanner, we first need to look back a bit in time to the work of Dr. Louis Sokoloff on radioactive tracers at the National Institute of Mental Health. For over thirty years, doctors have been using radioactive materials, called tracers, to help locate and treat medical problems. Before the advent of the CAT scanner, physicians often used tracers to make brain tumors show up in X rays. The resolution was only fair, nothing of the order of the CAT scan.

All organisms, ourselves included, use *glucose* as a basic fuel. Glucose is a sugar just like sucrose, the stuff we sprinkle over our cereal and buy at the grocery store for table sugar. However, we rarely take in glucose directly; rather, our bodies manufacture it from the food we eat. All cells, whether a muscle cell, a brain cell, or a heart

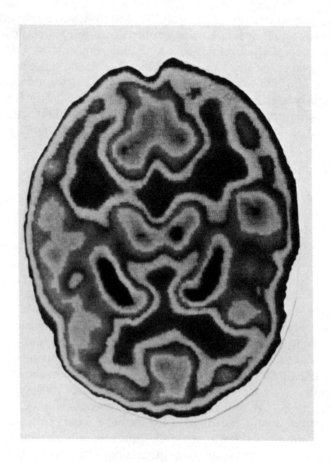

PETT scan of normal brain activity made on Ortec Neuro-ECAT scanner. Darkest areas represent the greatest activity. The notch is at the back of the head. (Courtesy Michael Phelps et al., Division of Biophysics, UCLA School of Medicine, Los Angeles, CA)

cell, require a constant supply of glucose just to keep from dying, just as a furnace, even on low, must have a constant supply of coal, gas, or oil to keep burning. In the morning, when we get up and turn up the heat, the furnace must, to meet this increased demand, have larger amounts of coal or oil. Likewise, a cell that becomes very active, as in a muscle that must lift and carry a weight, needs an increased supply of glucose. And brain cells are no exception.

When the neurons of the visual cortex respond to signals from the

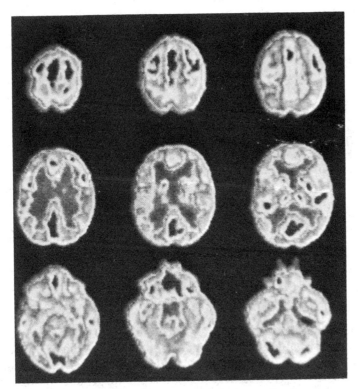

Series of PETT scans showing normal glucose use. Dark areas represent highest levels of activity. The backs of the heads are facing down. (Courtesy Michael Phelps et al., Division of Biophysics, UCLA School of Medicine, Los Angeles, CA)

eyes, they require a much larger quantity of glucose than when they are not active. If we could inject a radioactive form of glucose into the body and then stimulate one of the areas of the brain, this radioactive glucose would be absorbed by the nerve cells of that region. Unfortunately, it is not that easy. Glucose is used up too rapidly by the cell, and for a radioactive tracer to work, it must remain in the cells being studied. Brain tumors have little interaction with the cells around them, and so, once a tracer is in a tumor, it is there to stay. Not so with normal brain cells.

Dr. Sokoloff, however, discovered that active neurons could absorb a compound, *2-deoxyglucose,* just as they absorb glucose. Indeed, 2-deoxyglucose is chemically very similar to glucose, but once in the cell, it is trapped. So this glucose analog that has a radioactive carbon atom, C11, or a radioactive hydrogen atom, called tritium, will go straight to the working neurons, enter them, and remain for later analysis. Since Dr. Sokoloff performed his work before the invention of the PETT scanner, he used a process called *autoradiography.* In one of his experiments, he wished to see if the visual cortex was where the EEG had showed it to be. He injected a rat with the radioactive 2-deoxyglucose, waited the forty-five minutes needed for the tracer to be taken up by the neurons, killed the rat, and froze its brain. Then he sliced the frozen brain into thin sections, which he placed on photographic film. The radioactive tracer made an image on the film, and Sokoloff was able to tell that the 2-deoxyglucose had indeed ended up in the visual cortex of the rat's cerebrum. Sokoloff had made a major breakthrough. He was able to locate chemical operations within the brain. Unfortunately, however, he could not use this technique to study the human brain.

The PETT scanner changed all of that. This new machine was developed by Dr. Michael Ter-Pogossian in 1973 at Washington University Medical School in St. Louis. At first, just looking at a PETT scanner, you might think you are seeing a slightly modified CAT scanner. Like the computerized axial tomography, the PETT has a circular opening through which the patient, lying on a platform, is pushed. The information from this machine, like that from the CAT, is fed into a computer. The operators can have the computer print out the data or have it construct an image on a TV screen, and, just as with the CAT scanner, the image—the tomogram—shows a thin section of the brain that can be photographed. These similarities, however, are misleading. As one specialist insists, "the difference between the two scanners is very fundamental."

The PETT scanner, unlike the CAT scanner, does not use X rays. Indeed, mounted in that circular opening are a series of detectors, but not a single X-ray tube. What do these detectors pick up? And where do these emanations come from? The PETT looks for *gamma rays,* and the source of these gamma rays is the brain being scanned. Gamma rays are produced through the decay of radioactive substances. The human brain, however, does not naturally have any radioactive elements within it; they must be introduced. Subjects for PETT scanning are given an injection or asked to breathe in a small quantity of a radioactive tracer such as radioactive 2-deoxyglucose, Louis Sokoloff's tracer. As with Sokoloff's experiments, the tracer goes directly to the active neurons and stays there. Since, as Michael Phelps says, "the halflives of these tracers range from two minutes to no more than two hours, the exposure is short. That's good. By the time

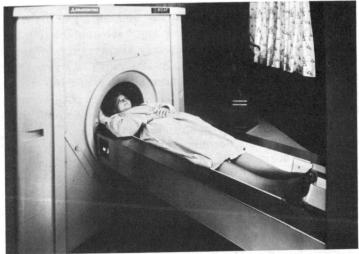

Patient being slid into Ortec Neuro-ECAT PETT scanner. (Courtesy E G & G Ortec)

you finish the procedure, the radioactivity is gone." Since gamma rays are a product of radioactive decay, we would expect that the neurons with the largest concentration of the tracer, the active cells, would throw out the greatest number of gamma rays. And so it is. Looking at the tomogram, we see areas giving off large numbers of these rays and areas giving off few if any.

If the PETT is picking up gamma rays, why then is it called a

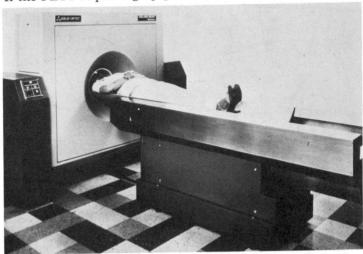

Patient undergoing positron emission scan by Ortec Neuro-ECAT scanner. (Courtesy E G & G Ortec)

positron emission tomography scanner and not a gamma ray emission tomography scanner? We obviously have another step here. In radioactive decay, before the gamma ray, there is the *positron,* which is a positively charged electron. In Chapter 1, we saw that electrons are negatively charged, and normally they are. But radioactive substances give off some odd particles of which the positively charged electron, the positron, is one. Positrons are few, electrons are many, and eventually a positron and an electron collide. When that happens, they destroy one another, releasing two gamma rays. So, a subject whose brain has been dosed with this radioactive tracer is constantly shooting off gamma rays. For the period of the examination, this person lies with his head inside the PETT (see Figure 7). The scanner measures, through its detectors, the number of these rays and feeds the figures into the computer. The computer then constructs the tomogram.

The tomogram of the PETT also differs from that of the CAT scanner. CAT scans are always in black and white, while PETT scans

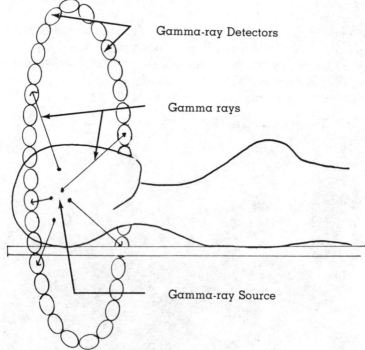

Figure 7.   PETT scanning process.

can be in color. Since the PETT is looking at activity in the brain, a researcher must be able to tell where that activity is. With a black and white tomogram, you are looking at shades of gray. At times this is satisfactory, but at others, the contrast is low. So, to make it clearer where the active regions are, color is added by the computer. The actual color codes vary from lab to lab. According to one PETT researcher, the choice of color "has no rationale. It is the whim of the individual researcher."

Although some specialists feel that the PETT has a real role in diagnosing brain disorders, it is also a major research tool. The information coming out of PETT research is as varied as the interests of the scientists involved. The PETT scanner has been used to look at everything from specialization within the cerebral hemispheres to epilepsy to visual response to schizophrenia. The doorway to the brain has been pushed open a little further, and through it, we see the dancing, multicolor PETT tomograms.

Another Scanner

The CAT scanner shows structure; the PETT scanner shows operation. In both instruments, however, the brain is subjected to a certain danger: X rays with the CAT and radioactive 2-deoxyglucose with the PETT. A new instrument, the *Nuclear Magnetic Resonance (NMR) scanner,* is able to develop images from the biochemical operations of the brain by merely creating a magnetic field around the subject being examined. Such a field is not as risky as exposure to X rays and does not require the introduction of chemicals such as 2-deoxyglucose.

The magnetic field allows the researcher or diagnostician to measure a property of hydrogen atoms called relaxation.

The length of relaxation depends on the type of compound in which hydrogen atoms are located. Thus, cerebrospinal fluid's relaxation time is three seconds, while that of blood is 300 milliseconds. So, if blood were in the cerebrospinal fluid, indicating some internal bleeding, the NMR could detect its presence and position. Tumor tissue also gives a different relaxation time than does normal brain tissue. Further, an NMR scan can tell the difference between malignant and benign tumors because of a difference in their relaxation time.

The NMR scanner is still in the experimental stage, and the

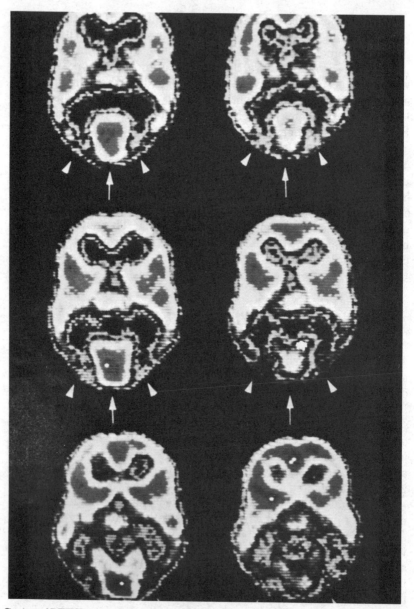

Series of PETT scans showing activity in the primary visual cortex, indicated by arrows. Column on right has the eyes closed. Subjects represented in the left column have their eyes open. Same "view" as in previous PETT scan. (Courtesy Michael Phelps et al., Division of Biophysics, UCLA School of Medicine, Los Angeles, CA)

possibilities for its use are still being discovered. However, researchers feel that it will be the new diagnostic machine of the future since it will be no more difficult or expensive to run than the CAT scanner and since, unlike the PETT, it does not require the use of specialized equipment like the cyclotron.

The whole trend in brain research has been to construct instruments by which the complexities of the brain can be studied so that researchers can understand how this organ does what it does. The instruments have not only been giving finer and more precise information about the workings of the brain, but they also are allowing scientists to probe the brain without disturbing it any more than is necessary.

But what is next? According to Dr. David Hubel, it is a method by which individual neurons may be watched from outside the skull "without drilling a hole in the skull." A full understanding of the workings of the brain is impossible without such a technique. Already, some work with microelectrodes has been done on the functioning of individual neurons, but such work requires that a foreign object be inserted into the brain. Two neurobiologists, Terence J. Sejnowski of Harvard Medical School and Stephen G. Reingold of Princeton University, have been able to do autoradiography experiments on single neurons. Like Sokoloff, they inject their mice with radioactive 2-deoxyglucose. They, however, use radioactive hydrogen instead of radioactive carbon as well as adding some additional steps to the procedure. The images they get show the individual neurons that have responded to light, sound, etc.

This is the first step toward non-invasive neuron research. What we need now is an instrument like the PETT scanner that can watch nerve cells, not just regions of the brain. Just when such a breakthrough will come, no one knows.

But remember, in 1970, just a little over a decade ago, no one could look at the operating brain.

For Further Thought

We talk glibly about how complex and complicated the brain is both in its structure and its function, yet, at every stage of brain research, we are tempted to simplify. Partially, this is done to help us understand what we are dealing with, but an even greater desire is the hope that finally we have some ultimate answer or solution. Unfortunately, reality seldom accommodates our wishes.

Take the neuron. In Chapter 1, we saw that nerve impulses travel from neuron to neuron, hitting first the dendrites and then passing on down through the axon to jump to the next dendrite. This is a simple picture that seems to satisfy our need to understand and to explain. But this simple model no longer works. Oh, this nerve cell model is correct, as far as it goes, but it doesn't go far enough.

Recent work at the National Institute of Health has revealed that nerve cells can also communicate with one another through their dendrites with one set of dendrites signaling another set. When dendrites are so activated, the whole network of fibers at that end of the neuron comes alive. Also, unlike axon to dendrite impulses which are either "on/off," these dendrite impulses can vary in strength, just as electric light bulbs can dim or brighten depending on the strength of the current. Neurologists have labeled these dendrite networks microcircuits. Such circuits probably see that the brain is not swamped with too much information at any one time.

No matter how many times we say that the brain is complicated, we never quite seem to say it with enough strength. Each stage of complexity yields to another. We seem determined to underestimate the most complicated object in our world, the one that rides in our very skulls.

3

Operating Through the Layers: The Functioning Brain

We live in a world of specialists. Look at the want ads. Companies no longer look for just toolmakers, but jig and fixture toolmakers or electro-optical-mechanical toolmakers. Industry doesn't just want engineers, but ditigal, analog, aerospace, or video engineers. And when was the last time you met a doctor who was a G.P. rather than an orthopedic surgeon or an ophthalmologist?

Like our society, our brains are composed of specialists, areas that control speech, sight, hearing, movement, and so on. By the middle of the nineteenth century, Paul Broca and Carl Wernicke had identified two distinct areas responsible for speech. A person with a damaged Broca center could no longer speak, while one with an injured Wernicke area spoke nonsense sentences.

The Double Brain

During the first half of the twentieth century, neurobiologists felt that one area of the brain could be trained to perform the function of another area, just as we might retrain a mechanical engineer to be a civil engineer. So, if you lost the use of one area of your brain, you could shift its functions to another area. The argument *seemed* logical. The brain has two cerebral hemispheres, which appear to be identical. So, why should we not assume that one hemisphere or the other could not completely duplicate the functions performed by the

61

other? If NASA can build computer backups for the space shuttle, why couldn't nature do the same with the human brain?

In 1844, a British doctor, A.L. Wigan, performed an autopsy on a friend who had died. Nothing about the dead man had been unusual during his life, nor had his death been noteworthy. Wigan, however, discovered that the man had only one cerebral hemisphere. Occasionally, either the right or the left cerebral hemisphere must be removed surgically because of severe brain damage or epilepsy. In some cases, patients recover much of the function of the missing hemisphere. Young children whose *Broca centers* are damaged can learn to speak anyway. Indeed, they may not show any speech problems whatever.

Although this sounds convincing, the brain generally is not this flexible, particularly in adults. Even in children, damage to either cerebral hemisphere is more or less permanent after the ages of nine or ten. In adults, if an area of the brain is destroyed or injured, its functions are generally not taken over by some other area of the brain. And, even when recovery occurs, such recovery is partial.

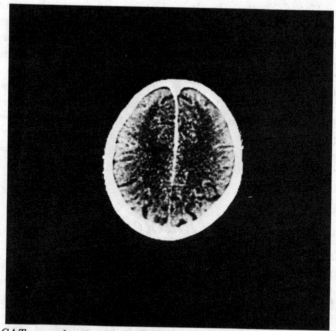

CAT scan showing right and left cerebral hemispheres. (Courtesy National Institute of Neurological and Communicative Disorders and Stroke)

Nor are the two cerebral hemispheres quite as similar as was once believed. In 1970, Norman Geschwind and Walter Levitsky of the Boston University School of Medicine measured the left and right cerebral hemispheres of some one hundred adult human brains. They found that in sixty-five percent of the brains the left hemisphere was larger than the right and, in eleven percent the right was larger. The major area of difference was near the hearing center, which, in the left cerebral hemisphere, corresponds to the *Wernicke speech center*. This region was one-third larger than in the opposite hemisphere.

The stage is now set for Dr. Roger Sperry, winner of the 1981 Nobel Prize in Medicine. It was Sperry who, in the 1960's, showed that the right and left cerebral hemispheres—the *right* and *left brain*—had distinctly different functions. These functions are not readily interchangeable between the two hemispheres. Sperry had introduced to the world the whole problem of the left brain-right brain.

Neurologists and physiologists had known for some time that the left cerebral hemisphere, the left brain, controls the right side of the body and the right cerebral hemisphere, the right brain, controls the left side. Why this crossover exists has not yet been answered, but exist it does. Thus, a right-handed person is dominated by his or her left brain, while a left-handed person is dominated by his or her right brain. When you cross your right leg over your left, you are acting under an impulse from the left side of your cerebrum. When your left ear picks up music from a speaker, the sound is transmitted to the right side of your cerebrum.

Most researchers prior to Sperry felt the two hemispheres to be duplicates, as we have seen. Damage to one could be corrected by training the other. The failure of such training didn't affect this belief. Obviously, even though the functions of the two halves of the brain may be different, the two hemispheres must have some way of coordinating their activity. Few of us feel that our brains are not unified, not acting as a coherent whole. We do not feel any battle between the left and right hemispheres, and when we perform an action such as walking, we do so in complete confidence that our brain will keep our right and left legs from getting out of synch. Thus, the two cerebral hemispheres must communicate. And they do so through a bundle of fibers called the corpus callosum (see Figure 1). The corpus callosum lies like a bridge between the right and left brain, carrying signals from one side to the other so that our right hand does know what our left hand is doing. Cut the corpus callosum, and the communication between the right and left hemispheres

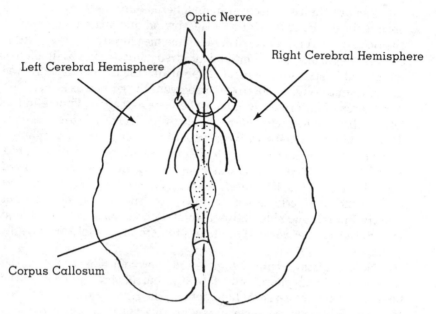

Figure 1. Dr. Roger Sperry studied patients whose corpus callosum and optic nerves had been severed surgically. The broken line shows the scalpel's path.

should cease. Indeed, this is exactly what happens.

Researchers cannot cut the corpus callosum in a human brain just to see what will happen. Medical ethics and human considerations rightly prevent such experiments. However, some epileptics suffer from such severe seizures that, even under medication, their lives are threatened. For such people, the final solution is the cutting of the corpus callosum so that the seizure is localized rather than spreading explosively to both cerebral hemispheres. In most such cases, the surgery prevents further widespread seizures.

Sperry made a study of a number of these surgically-severed corpus callosum cases. Whereas before each patient had a single, unified mind, now each appeared to have two independent minds. As Sperry noted, both the right and left brains have their own sensations and abilities. Thus, when the two halves of our brains cannot communicate, they still function, but independently and in different ways.

This is not to say that the autonomy of the right and left brains in the subjects studied by Sperry is grossly obvious. It is not. In fact, initially nothing of this split was suspected. The patients' personalities were much as they had been before their operations:

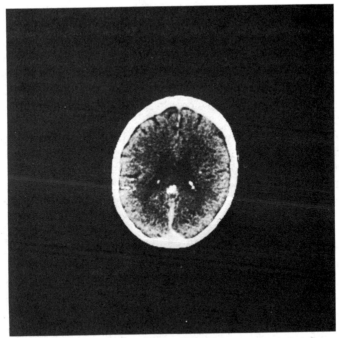

CAT scan showing corpus callosum linking right and left cerebral hemispheres. (Courtesy National Institute of Neurological and Communicative Disorders and Stroke)

neither their intelligence nor their ability to deal with the world around them was apparently affected. However, each of these patients favored his or her right side. Indeed, put a pencil into the patient's left hand and he or she paid it no attention. Such patients also showed no reaction hitting something with their left side. They seemed to be reacting with only their left brains.

An experiment was set up to test these observations in which a line of lights was strung and designed so that each bulb flashed individually from left to right. Subjects whose corpus callosum had been cut were asked to tell which flashing lights they could see. All of them could see the lights on the right, but not those on the left. At first, the researchers thought these people were blind in the left eye. However, when asked to point to the lights they could see flashing, each subject pointed to the lights both to the right and to the left. Why were they unable to say they saw the left-hand lights?

The speech centers of the brain, both Broca's and Wernicke's, are located in the left cerebral hemisphere, the left brain. When asked about visual impulses to the left brain, the subjects above could answer since the left brain controls speech. However, since the right brain is cut off from access to the left brain and, therefore, from access to the speech centers, these patients had no way of saying they could indeed see the left-hand lights. But, since both halves of the brain can control hand movements—the right brain, the left hand; the left brain, the right hand—these people could indicate what they saw by pointing.

We see, therefore, one of the major differences between the left and right brain, speech. In the years since these initial experiments, much has been learned about the working of both halves of the cerebrum. Additional research has also shown that our personalities and our abilities are affected and determined by the dominance of our left or right brain. Are you good at solving problems? Do you find it easy to speak and write? Then your left brain is dominant, and you are probably right-handed (see Figure 2). The left brain is verbal and analytical. It can be simulated by a computer. Do you paint or draw well? Do you find it easier to deal with the visual rather than the verbal? Then your right brain dominates, and you are probably left-handed. The right brain is non-verbal, but is good at detecting spatial relationships. It cannot be simulated by a computer.

The dominance of either the left or right brain does not mean that we do not have the use of both hemispheres. Indeed, Dr. Marcel Kinsbourne of the Hospital for Sick Children in Toronto feels that both hemispheres are used in the imaginative and speculative processes.

Knowing that this difference between right and left brain exists does have practical benefits. Doing two things at once is something we all try occasionally. Sometimes the attempt works. Most people can simultaneously drive and have a conversation. Few of us, however, can read and watch TV at the same time. If two tasks can be done together, they are generally controlled by different hemispheres. Two that cannot be done together are functions of the same hemisphere. In a simple test, Marcel Kinsbourne illustrated these conclusions by having several children learn to balance a small metal rod on the index fingers of both their left and right hands. He then had them recite a series of memorized phrases. None of the children had any trouble keeping the rod balanced on the left finger while repeating the phrases. Shifting to the right hand, however, the children suddenly found balancing the rod difficult. Speaking and control of the right hand are functions of the left brain. The right brain, however, controls the left hand. So, if you try to do two tasks that are controlled by the same cerebral hemisphere, you will find one inter-

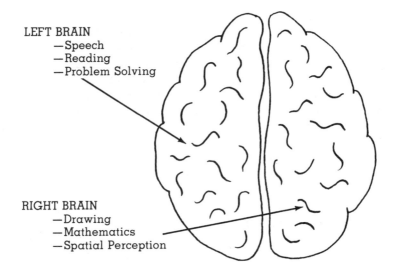

LEFT BRAIN
  —Speech
  —Reading
  —Problem Solving

RIGHT BRAIN
  —Drawing
  —Mathematics
  —Spatial Perception

Figure 2. Major areas of difference between the right and left brain.

fering with the other. You can effectively do them only if they are functions of different hemispheres.

If we can find out what the right brain does and what the left brain does, we will know what jobs can be done at the same time and what cannot. The simple knowledge that the right half of the body is controlled by the left brain and the left side by the right brain can help in physical operations.

Little interference can be found between movements of the right hand and left foot and between the left hand and the right foot. Using this information NASA has designed control panels for astronauts in which an astronaut can perform two operations with either the right hand-left foot or left hand-right foot. In this way, the time of complicated operations is almost halved. What can work for NASA can also work for industry. Machine operators can do twice as many tasks in half the time. Even something as simple as operating a duplicating machine could be speeded up if the operation button was a foot control. The hands could then be used just to change pages.

But this is only the start. Both left and right brain have their own skills, and both can be educated independently of the other. In mice, researchers have anesthetized one cerebral hemisphere. They have then trained the conscious one to run a maze. Later, they would put the trained half-brain asleep. The now-conscious hemisphere could not run the original maze, but it could be taught to run another maze.

Eventually, when some simple and harmless method of putting

one half of our brain to sleep is developed, we will be able to double our skills by educating each hemisphere separately. Imagine a court reporter who, during a trial, could dictate a story while simultaneously sketching judge, jury, and defendant for the six o'clock news. As Dr. J. Eric Holmes has observed, with such training of both halves of our brain, we may be able to double our population, increasing our pool of needed skills, without affecting our food supply.

We have all heard psychologists talk about how each of us possesses hidden fears. We have also been told that we often refuse to remember the unpleasant things that happen to us, yet we are told these unpleasant memories are still within our minds. Indeed the whole purpose of psychoanalysis is to uncover both these hidden fears and memories so that we can learn what is at the core of our anxieties. But where are these fears and memories kept? Sigmund Freud called this area the unconscious, but neither he nor anyone else has been able to say where in the brain the unconscious is located, at least until now.

The right brain, the non-verbal cerebral hemisphere, may be Freud's unconscious. Certainly, if your mind wished to put some bit of information out of your verbal reach, it could find no better place than the right hemisphere. This hemisphere has no way of communicating since the speech center is in the left brain. The right brain, however, is able to see spatial relationships, and, perhaps by devising some sort of artistic code, psychologists could reach the right brain and could discover the secrets of the unconscious. Such discoveries might lead to dramatic treatments of various mental illnesses such as paranoia and schizophrenia.

The right brain may also hold the answer to some very strange questions. For instance, what are ghosts? A stroke patient wakes up in the middle of the night. She is convinced that someone else is in the room with her. She sees and hears no one else, but her feeling that she isn't alone persists. Despite the partial paralysis of her left arm and leg, she gets out of bed and wanders through the house. She finds no one, but she is sure that just off to her left is another presence. Other stroke victims are sure that someone is in the bed with them. They look to the left and see an arm or a leg that belongs to that other person. Ghosts? In a way, yes. All of these people have had strokes affecting their right brain. The right brain is involved in the maintenance of our self-identity. Damage to it results in a person no longer being able to recognize the existence of his or her left side. The person still vaguely senses the presence of the left half of his body, but does not consciously realize it belongs to him and is a part of him. Instead, it becomes a ghostly presence off to the left, or it becomes an arm or a leg belonging to someone else, another patient, even the doctor. Damage to the left brain produces no similar sensation. Instead, the person generally has problems with speaking and writing, depending on the extent of the injury, but there is no ghostly presence to the right.

What else the study of the right and left brain will tell us, we can't say yet. But in learning about the specialists in our brain, we are learning about the basics of how and why our brains function the way they do.

Sex and the Brain

Looking at the double mind has led researchers into one of the most controversial subjects of the latter half of the twentieth century. Coming out of these studies is evidence that differences do exist between the functioning of the brains of men and women. Such findings, though apparently valid, are misleading because the idea of difference has come to mean either that something or someone is superior or inferior. Actually, the whole business of superiority/ inferiority rarely has anything to do with being different. We all recognize the differences in ability between an engineer and a painter, between a painter and a psychologist. Yet we can't claim that one is superior to the other; they are just different. As Dr. Diane McGuinness of Stanford University observes, "People say if you're different you can't be equal, which of course, is nonsense. It's a problem in logic that crops up too frequently. Different is different. A white person and a black person have different colored skin. No amount of argument is going to turn the black person white or the white person black. That is a fact. Whether they are equal in terms of the law and opportunity is an entirely different issue."

Furthermore, when we speak of the differences between the workings of men's and women's brains, we are not speaking of specific individuals, but of two generalized groups. Individual variation is so great that no one person is going to conform to the general characteristics of his or her class. Jerre Levy, one of the leading researchers of sexual differentiation, has pointed out that the greatest percentage—eighty to ninety percent—of differences among people are found within men and within women. By recognizing the truth in Levy's statement, the importance of this difference between men's and women's brains shrinks to a reasonable and realistic level.

What we can gain from our knowledge of these differences is a chance to provide an equal opportunity to every member of our society. Equality requires that everyone has the same chance, and by ignoring basic character traits, we ignore the needs of a large part of society. Both men as well as women suffer from this neglect.

Genetically, men and women are the same except for one *chromosome,* the carrier of the genetic material *DNA.* Sex is determined by the combination of X and Y chromosomes. Females have two X's, while males have one X and one Y.

Physically, we know what differences exist between men and women, which are caused by the presence of a chemical in males, *testosterone,* and in females of a chemical, *estrogen.* Every fetus begins as a female. If estrogen is present, it remains a female. If testosterone is present, it changes the female reproductive system, making it into the male system. All men have the remnants of ovaries.

These chemicals also act upon the brain. Until recently, the only site for this interaction was thought to be the hypothalamus, the site of our sex drive. But George Ojemann, a Seattle neurosurgeon, has discovered from working with epileptics that the language centers in men and women, although both in the left hemisphere, have slightly different configurations. Also, an Israeli researcher, Ruben Gur, using a radioactive tracer, has discovered that the brains of men and women operate differently and are supplied by blood differently when doing various tasks.

Roger Gorski of UCLA has found that the shapes of the cells in the hypothalamus in male and female rats are different (see Figure 3). By looking at a slide, you can tell from which sex the cell came. Although no one has dissected the human brain for such cells, scientists feel certain that the same differences would be found between men and women. As Donald Paff of Rockefeller University has observed, each layer of our brain represents that of a lower order, running from fish to lizard to mammal. So, what is true of one animal's brain in our evolutionary ancestry should be true of us.

Pfaff has also done work on finding receptor sites for estrogen and testosterone in other parts of a rat's brain besides the hypothalamus. He found such sites in the cerebrum. These sites, initially, do not seem to prefer one chemical over the other. However, once either estrogen or testosterone binds with the receptor site, that site is no longer open to the other chemical.

Our sexual chemicals, therefore, do not just change the characteristics of our bodies, but also of our brains. Except for the appearance of the secondary sexual traits at puberty, this sexual differentiation of both body and brain, according to Diane McGuinness, is generally complete at birth. We would, therefore, expect to see differ-

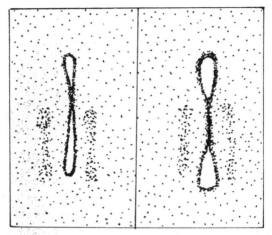

Figure 3.   Artist's representation of difference between cell clusters found in the hypothalamus of female rats (left) and male rats (right).

ences in the reactions of newly-born boys and girls, and indeed we do.

Tests run on female babies show that their senses of hearing and touch develop more quickly than do these senses in male babies. Sight, however, develops more rapidly in boys. Thus, girls tend to react to sounds around them, particularly to music and voices; boys are more interested in colors and three-dimensional objects. These differences remain throughout the life of each child. Girls begin making sounds and finding comfort in voices earlier than boys. Boys begin more quickly to explore their surroundings, touching and handling anything that they can reach. In women, the end result is a facility with language, both spoken and written. Men's ability is to deal analytically with spatial relationships and with math.

Women then, in general, make more use of their left cerebral hemisphere, and men of their right. Again, let us remember, we are talking about the average abilities in each group, not about individual men and women. But why this difference?

David Shucard, a Denver biologist, conjectures that the presence of testosterone may delay the development of the left hemisphere in the fetus of boys. Thus, female fetuses would have a head start in the use of their left brain, and boys would be forced to rely more on their right brains. Also, according to Doreen Kimura of Western Ontario's

University Hospital, men have traditionally been more dependent on their right brain than women. For much of our species' history, we have been a hunter-gatherer society. The hunters, generally men, had to be able to judge distances so they could throw spears and hunting clubs. If they didn't do this well, the tribe starved. Such an ability demands a good spatial sense—the ability to see objects in relation to one another—and is the province of the right brain.

Many researchers such as Jerre Levy of the University of Chicago feel that women, unlike men, show less distinction between their right and left brains. Evidence for this comes from studies of victims of tumors and strokes. Doreen Kimura, who examined tumors and strokes affecting the left brain in both men and women, found that women were not often as impaired as men. Even women who suffered speech problems seemed to recover more of their speaking ability more often than men. George Ojemann found that stimulating any part of the male's left hemisphere with electrodes caused a language block. But, in women, the block only arose when very specific areas of the left brain were stimulated. Again, using the hunter-gatherer analogy, Kimura offers an explanation of this resiliency in women. Since women did not have to develop the spatial ability in the right brain to the same extent as men, they could devote more neurons to language skills. Women, therefore, may have back-up speech centers in the right brain.

Another possible factor is puberty. Deborah Waber of Harvard Medical School has found that the right and left brain are less specialized in people reaching puberty early. Girls generally arrive at puberty about two years before boys.

Being less specialized, the two halves of women's brains are in closer touch. Men are more isolated in their right hemisphere. Since this hemisphere is non-verbal, men often have problems communicating (particularly their emotions) with others. Women are not plagued so much with this problem. Further, their more unified double mind may be able to assemble information more quickly than men, which may be, according to Levy, the source of what we call female intuition.

In the future, doctors, debating whether to operate to remove a tumor or an epileptic center, may have to take a patient's sex into account. Women with their less specialized hemispheres would make better candidates for such surgery. Any damage to a woman's brain may not be permanent.

Yet, perhaps, one of the most important results of this recognition of the differences in the brains of men and women is its impact on education. Our schools traditionally rely on lectures given by teachers to students sitting in rows of chairs. This arrangement favors young girls since, with their enhanced hearing, they learn by asking questions and by listening to what others have to say. Voice tones and intensity are also important to girls when learning. The need for boys, however, to move around, to touch, and to examine is rarely given an outlet in the school. Boys, with their reliance on sight, prefer to go out and look at their world. They learn, therefore, by touching and examining more than by listening to explanations.

Because schools cater to the left brain abilities of girls, Carol Nagly Jacklin and Eleanor Maccoby of Stanford discovered that girls are actually more intellectually independent and aggressive than boys. Indeed, boys are generally intellectually timid and anxious. Ironically, many of the standardized tests used to check ability and learning are slanted in favor of the boys. Such examinations as the National Merit Scholarship Examination give a distinct edge to any-one who has a strong spatial sense. No one will argue that many technical professions such as physics and engineering require a strong facility with math. Yet, even nontechnical professions in which math is rarely if ever used, such as law, use tests that discrimi-nate against those who are poor in math. Thus, women often find it difficult to get past such tests that lead to law school and other nontechnical training and professions.

By recognizing the different needs of girls and boys, men and women, we could easily correct the problems boys have in the early grades, and we could give girls an equal chance at showing their abilities. By bringing our testing more in line with what is actually required, we can also prevent the exclusion of talented women from jobs they are actually well-equipped to handle. The differences we see are not great, but they are significant. Differing abilities present different problems and require different solutions.

What we have here is the possibility then of fully developing the intellectual abilities of both men and women. We do not have a further argument for the superiority of one sex over the other.

Challenge to the Double Brain

No recent theory of how the brain works has so attracted the atten-tion and interest not only of neurobiologists but of the general public as the double-mind theory. The idea of the double mind is appealing since it seems to fit with the way the brain looks, cerebrum and cerebellum being divided down the middle. Also, it provides some reasonable explanations for how the brain carries out its functions.

Yet, despite these attractions, the left brain-right brain theory is not without its critics. One is an English psychologist, Stan Gooch, who has studied several patients with one whole cerebral hemisphere removed surgically. Such an operation is rare, but occasionally one of the hemispheres is so badly damaged that leaving it in the skull poses more dangers through malfunction than removing it.

We might assume from what we have been learning about the double mind that such an operation would leave the patient missing part of his or her skills and abilities. Gooch, however, found this was not the case. One man, whose left brain was removed due to the presence of a large tumor, was able to speak and sing songs within six months of the surgery. A woman Gooch examined also had her left hemisphere removed to eliminate paralyzing epileptic fits. Within a short period of time, she was reading and felt confident enough to go out and find a job. Neither patient seems to have suffered any problems with controlling his or her right side.

Gooch does not feel that the double-mind idea is entirely wrong. He does feel that the two cerebral hemispheres are more flexible than we have given them credit for being. This flexibility is called into play when, as in the case of a removal of one or the other hemisphere, the brain has no choice but to adapt. Also, if you remember back to the early part of the chapter, you will recall that in the nineteenth century, a British doctor discovered that a friend had been born without two cerebral halves. This man functioned normally all his life.

Do these cases mean that the double-mind theory is incorrect? Not necessarily. First, we know that the flexibility Gooch supposes to exist does in fact exist in children through the ages of nine or ten. As we noted earlier, through this age, children can learn to duplicate the actions of a damaged cerebral hemisphere. However, with age this flexibility of the brain disappears to a great extent just as flexibility of the joints vanishes with age. However, if the brain has no choice, as with the removal of one side or the other of the cerebrum, it should be able to rediscover this flexibility without violating the double-brain theory.

Further, as we saw in our discussion of the sexual differences between the brains of men and women, women's cerebral hemispheres are not so rigidly specialized as men's. They show, as Doreen Kimura's studies revealed, a marked ability to relearn functions lost through damage or surgery. And, since we said that individual men and women vary greatly, some men are bound to possess this same brain flexibility. Is the split brain theory wrong? By no means, but like all theories, it requires modification from time to time. Theories are constructed on the information at hand. When that information changes or new information comes to light, you do not throw out the old ideas unless they are proven to be dead wrong. Instead, you see what the new data tells you about the old.

So, let's look at research being done by EEG Systems Laboratory in San Francisco, which has been working for years to develop new and more sophisticated EEG equipment as well as methods for interpreting those results (see the Alan Gevins interview, Chapter 2). Satisfied with the reliability of their instruments and techniques, the researchers at EEG Systems Laboratory started to see what they could learn about the brain's operations. Would they see area specialization as proposed by Sperry and others? Yes and no. Or perhaps yes, no, no, and yes would describe the sequence of events more accurately.

Alan Gevins, director of the lab, and his colleagues tested a group of people, having them perform several tasks, including arranging colored blocks to form a design; writing clear, coherent sentences; and just scribbling. Theoretically, the left cerebral hemisphere should have lit up more for writing sentences than for arranging blocks, and it did. But, there was no difference of any sort between writing sentences and scribbling. This suggested that the brain wave patterns were reflecting finger movements rather than thinking.

In a second experiment, the researchers measured brain waves during mental block rotations, arithmetic, and letter substitution tasks. No finger movement was required, and the tasks were equally difficult. Surprise. The entire cerebrum was active, and the patterns of electrical responses seemed to be fairly uniform. Neither hemisphere showed relatively more activity than the other during any of these controlled tasks.

In a third experiment, the EEG Systems Laboratory used a new type of analysis to measure fraction-of-a-second changes in brain waves while people played numerical and spatial versions of a very controlled video game. With this more powerful method, the scientists saw a rapidly changing mosaic of electrical patterns for both tasks. Specialized activity appeared and disappeared in a sixth of second, but such specialized activity was only a small detail in a very complex pattern involving differences between all sixteen recorded areas of the brain.

To make the story complete, the researchers performed a fourth experiment, in which two types of spatial judgments were compared, one with and one without finger movement. They also developed a more refined version of their analysis that allowed only the areas of greatest contrast to be seen—much like removing the gray tones from a photograph so that it is all black and white. About a third of a second after the stimulus appeared, only the right parietal area of the brain showed difference in activity between the two types of spatial judgment (when this area is damaged, a patient can't find his way around the ward and has other problems with spatial orientation). About a half second after the stimulus appeared, people began to express their answer by moving their finger in one version of the experiment. Now, only the left motor area showed an activity difference. The switch from right to left hemispheres took only a sixth of a second.

According to Gevins, former research that found speech centers, hearing centers, vision centers, and so on was not wrong. It just did not go far enough, or was not able to go far enough. Gevins' EEG lab is a scientific and technological pointman in brain research. "My idea, at the moment," he says, "is that the brain is like a computer network with thousands of processors. Some handle very specific functions such as the feature analyzers of the visual cortex that are 'hardwired' to pull out certain angles, different patterns of movement, and so forth from the field of vision. On the other hand, we have certain functions like long-term memory which don't seem to be localized in any one area. And there are all the gradations in between." For Gevins, the important thing is finding out how all of these operations are coordinated and how they interact with one another.

So, we have a view of the brain that says it is a mass of circuits and many of the traditional control areas are components in those circuits. This doesn't mean the component is the circuit, but if you pull it out by injuring it, you can stop the circuit.

The Triple Brain

Still, we seem to need more than a theory of the double brain to explain the functioning of our brains. Dr. Paul MacLean of the National Institute of Mental Health offers us another partial answer. He feels that the human brain has three distinct layers and that these layers are both chemically and structurally quite different as well as evolutionarily separate and distinct. The outermost of these three layers MacLean calls the *neomammalian* (see Figure 4). It is the same as the cerebrum, which, as we saw in Chapter 1, is the location of conscious, intellectual thought. The second layer is the *paleomammalian* or the limbic system. This structure is the source of emotions. The third layer and the deepest is the reptilian or *R-complex*. This formation controls instinctive behavior. The R-complex is surrounded by the limbic system which, in turn, is surrounded by the neomammalian layer.

Nothing about the triple brain contradicts findings about the right-left brain, and MacLean's theory complements Sperry's double brain. Indeed, the double brain is merely the two hemispheres that make up the cerebrum or the neomammalian, one part of MacLean's triple brain.

MacLean has used his theory of the triple brain to look at irrational behavior. We all like to think of ourselves as rational, and we even differentiate humanity from other species by calling ourselves "the rational animals." Yet a good deal of our behavior is anything but rational. When MacLean uses the term irrational, he means an act that does not come about through a series of logically reasoned steps. You meet someone you dislike. What is your physical reaction? You notice your movements are abrupt, and you keep your arms and hands close to your body. In short, you physically close the other person off from yourself. Your actions are not a result of conscious decisions. You act so without thought, which is irrational. You cannot claim you arrived at your conclusion through reason. Instead, your body movement is instinctive.

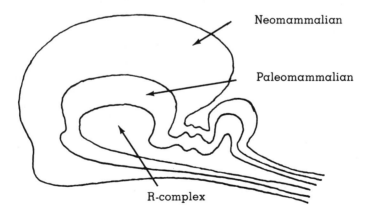

Figure 4. The triple brain.

According to MacLean, instinctive behavior is a product of the R-complex. This part of the triple brain, which is closest to the brain stem, is the most primitive, and MacLean discovered that much of the R-complex's activity corresponds to reptilian behavior. Reptiles are almost solely creatures of ritual. Their behavior is programmed so that any member of a reptile species will react the same way as any other member of that species. When two males of the common fence lizard meet, they both begin bobbing their heads and doing aggressive push-ups in the same way. Anyone who has seen monkeys at a zoo knows that they too have such ritualistic responses. Squirrel monkeys establish a pecking order through a high-pitched cry and a spreading of the thighs. When MacLean cut out a portion of the R-complex of several squirrel monkeys, he found they no longer went through this ritual.

MacLean, himself, realizes that traditionally we dismiss instinct as affecting human behavior. Still, at least some of our actions seem to be instinctive. Anyone who has worked in an office or business knows that, besides the official hierarchy, an unofficial pecking order exists. When we cannot look back at what someone else has done, we are uneasy about making decisions or in taking action. These are both examples of human instinctive behavior. Often our instincts are in conflict with out conscious intentions. Or, as MacLean would have it, the programming of the R-complex and the neomammalian, the cerebrum, are contradictory.

Upon meeting that person you dislike, you try to be polite, You make small talk about the weather, business, or sports. Your body, however, is delivering another message, saying *I don't like you. I don't want to be near you.* So, despite your conscious attempts, tension grows, and both of you become uncomfortable.

Whether we can change our instinctive behavior, control our R-complexes, or not is unknown. We can, however, recognize its existence and recognize that our instincts are often at odds with our words. Whenever possible, we can try to minimize the gap between our cerebrum and our R-complex, thus cutting down on our discomfort in some social situations.

This balance in the brain is not that simple because it is not just a two-way, but rather a three-way balance. The second layer of MacLean's triple brain, the limbic system, also affects behavior. Like the R-complex, the limbic system does not operate on logic and reason. Instead, it acts on emotion. Every day we react and act upon feelings. We immediately like this person, we think our job interview will go badly, we know that the next bus is going to be late. Rain isn't in the forecast, but we take an umbrella anyway. The emotional response to that person you dislike is your dislike, and it is a product of the limbic system. Sometimes you can explain why this particular person is disagreeable, and sometimes you can't. In either case, you are being directed by your limbic system. If you can say why you dislike this person, you have used your cerebrum to supply the reasons for your emotional response. Your dislike comes before your justification.

As far back as 1939, the limbic system had been tagged as the seat of emotion. Two University of Chicago researchers, Kluver and Bucey, destroyed part of the limbic system in a monkey. Whereas before the monkey reacted violently to being handled, now it no longer cared. Its only response was docility.

The connection between the limbic system and emotion was demonstrated even more dramatically in studies of epilepsy. Epileptic discharges in the limbic system cause definite emotional responses. A patient of Doctor Richard Restak had an epileptic attack in a restaurant. This man, who was normally pleasant and understanding, grew violently angry at the waiter because he felt his steak smelled horribly and wasn't cooked enough. He repeated his complaint with two other steaks before collapsing with a seizure. In another instance, a woman would periodically sense a breeze, as though someone had walked by. Even though she knew no one was there, she had to look. Like the man above, this woman was having epileptic discharges in her limbic system. Her response differed, but it was no less emotional.

Without the limbic system, we would find ourselves acting with the mechanical ritualism of the R-complex. We would lack the nuances that most of us find most exciting in life. Unlike reptiles, we don't merely find a mate or automatically fit ourselves into a position within society. Instead, we feel that this man or this woman is right or wrong and that we like or don't like how others treat us.

But the limbic system, as with the entire triple brain, makes trouble for us. Much of our internal conflict comes from the contradictory messages the three layers of the brain send out. When you are in the presence of that person you dislike, the conflicting intentions of cerebrum, limbic system, and R-complex make you uncomfortable. When you finally get away from that person, you are relieved as your three brain layers no longer need to contradict one another, and the strain of that internal opposition disappears.

The R-complex and the limbic system cause an automatic reaction to people and situations. Obviously, such response has its advantages when you need to make a quick decision. However, when you have time to consider that decision, you should attempt to counter or at least to analyze what your R-complex and limbic system are telling you. Most of us claim to vote for a candidate because we like what he has to say about current political issues. Yet, at the same time, most of us know that political speeches are often written to say as little as possible, and we rarely expect a candidate's campaign promises to be carried out. So, what is it that most of us use to decide our vote? Our reactions to the person. The ones we vote for give us the right signs to appeal to our R-complex. With our reptilian third brain appeased, our limbic system feels that this man or woman is right for us. With two thirds of the triple brain satisfied, the cerebrum has no problems in supplying justifications for our decision.

Our decision may be right, but we should realize that it is not really based upon the rational logic of our cerebrum. It is based instead upon the non-reasoning parts of our brain. Therefore, whenever possible, we should look closely at our decisions and ask ourselves whether they really are the best course of action. We should always remember that two thirds of our brain is influenced by other factors than logic, and we should check those factors and see if they are indeed valid. If they are not, we should ignore the R-complex and the limbic system.

AEP

When we are considering theories of how the brain works, we are really developing models for the electrical activity of the brain. The researchers at the EEG Systems Laboratory are probably undertaking one of the most sophisticated investigations of the patterns such electrical activity produces. These scientists are attempting to find the specific pattern associated with every function of the brain. Just as each of us has a unique set of fingerprints, so, in theory, each activity of the brain produces a uniquely individual EEG recording.

As early as the 1930's, biologists and doctors had discovered that a single stimulus such as a flashing light or a ringing bell would produce on an EEG a response called the evoked potential or evoked response. The evoked potential would be detected in the part of the cerebrum associated with the sense being tested, the vision center for light and the hearing center for sound. The initial research used unconscious animals because the brains of conscious animals produced so much background noise from movement, breathing, and so on that the evoked potential was drowned out. In 1951, a British scientist developed a method to isolate the evoked potential. He would repeat a stimulus many times and then make EEG recordings during each repetition. Laboriously, he would compare all the EEG's, subtracting background noise. The common factor left was the evoked potential, called in this case the *average evoked potential (AEP)*.

Let us say you want to find the AEP for a flashing light. You

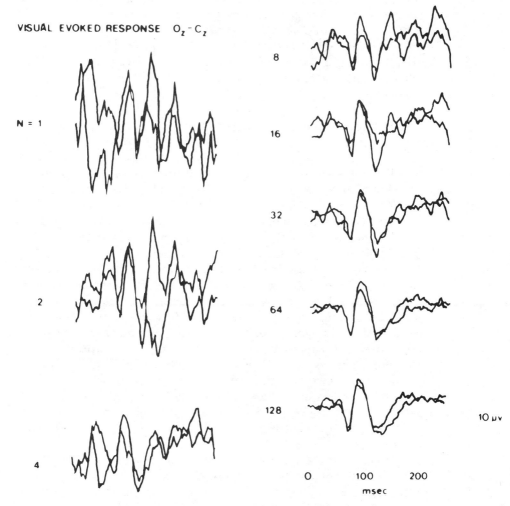

Computer averaging of the evoked potential for a visual stimulus to arrive at the AEP. The first shows a single response. The last shows the final pattern after 128 trials. 10 μv = 0.00001 volt (ten one-millionths of a volt); 100 msec = 0.1 second (one-tenth of a second). (Courtesy Nicolet Biomedical Instruments)

would shine that light into a conscious person's eyes some 200 times. At the same time, you would make an EEG recording for each flash of the light. Then, after averaging, you would have the AEP located in the visual cortex for that particular stimulus.

The advent of the computer made all of this a great deal easier and quicker. Indeed, one researcher feels that, for investigating the operation of the brain, "computer analysis seems to have been most productive." But the computer brought more than just speed and efficiency to EEG research. It brought new information. Specifically, it brought to light a stimulus response, P300.

Alan Gevins tell us that "P300 is a major peak of the AEP, and it is still exciting researchers after more than a decade." What is the source of this excitement? Gevins explains that "It was the first peak to be found in the AEP that could reasonably be identified with some mental activity, although a very narrowly defined one. It seems to be a sign that a person has perceived something novel, something unusual, and is updating his mental set. You could use the P300 as an unusual event detector." Well, what can be done with P300? Is it merely an interesting curiosity or can it produce something useful?

One proposal is to use P300 to test the ability of people such as military officers to make good, sound decisions. If we could tell which people were actually capable of making decisions and which weren't, we might well increase the efficiency of everything from the military to the federal government to the local city council.

Dr. Marta Kutas of the University of Illinois found that a person asked to push a button would show P300 just before he or she actually hit the button. If, however, the person did not consciously decide to push the button, but did so impulsively, no P300 appeared. But, perhaps of most importance, if that person made an error in pushing the button, P300 appeared. It did so, not before the button pushing but after. The recognition of the mistake brings P300, but such recognition follows the act; it does not precede it. So, we have three possible reactions in relation to P300. P300's appearance before an action shows a conscious decision, its non-appearance reveals an impulsive, non-conscious act, and its appearance after an act shows a mistake.

This sounds promising. But how could it be used? Imagine a military commander who wants to determine which of his junior officers should be promoted. Now, he would evaluate the reports of those commanders they had served under. He would probably still do that, but, in our not-too-distant future, he could also check their ability to make quick, accurate, conscious decisions, certainly of importance in an officer. So, he sends each officer to the base psychologist who rigs them up to an EEG and gives them an advanced version of Kutas's button-pushing exercise. Those who make conscious, correct decisions will show P300 before each such decision. Those who act impulsively will show no P300. And those who cannot make proper decisions will have P300's showing up after their mistakes.

When such testing might be possible is a question of time, but the overall work with AEP has produced some present day benefits in a new discipline called *neurometrics*. The AEP's for any particular region of the brain are distinctive and recognizable. They are, if we wish, the fingerprints of brain activity. If we compare AEP's for the sensory cortex of several normal brains of the same age, we see that they are the same. Neurometrics uses this similarity of AEP's to check for problems in a person's brain. If a doctor suspects that an area of a subject's brain has been affected by a tumor, stroke, or epilepsy, he can check the AEP of various regions of the patient's brain and match them against the AEP's from normal brains. Where the AEP's are different is where damage and problems will be.

But why stop here? If we can record normal brain wave patterns on magnetic tape, why can't we feed them back into the brain? Such feedback has already been done with alpha waves. Since alpha waves are an idling signal for the brain, feeding them back into the brain helps people relax: the ultimate tranquilizer, without, as far as we know, any side effects. This technique could not be used to feed normal brain wave signals back into a person and cure him or her of epilepsy or Parkinson's disease since here we are talking about a physical cause for the disorders. Yet perhaps normal patterns could be fed back into stroke-affected brains to teach them some of the tasks the stroke has erased from the brain's memory. Perhaps it would stimulate other regions of the brain to mimic these signals, and thus stroke victims might recover some of their lost abilities. Of course with more complicated patterns being discovered and recorded, we may be able to feed back a wave pattern for, say, concentration. We could teach our brains to concentrate by imitating this pattern.

Building a Brain

In addition to creating theories and measuring and recording electrical activity in the brain, a third method exists for learning about the brain's operations: building a brain. Unfortunately, neither our knowledge nor our technology is up to such a task. The closest we can

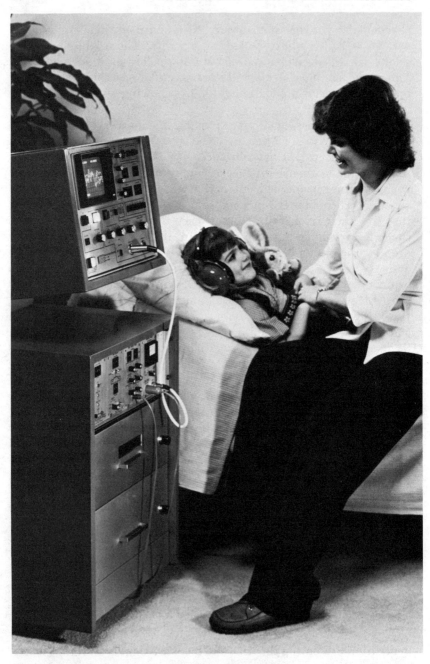

Nicolet Instruments DC-2000 recording AEP for an auditory test of a young girl. (Courtesy Nicolet Biomedical Instruments)

THE CYCLING BRAIN

The brain doesn't function at a uniform pace. According to Michael Chase of the UCLA School of Medicine, our brains go through a ninety-minute cycle. Our ability to think clearly and concisely as well as our ability to create and to imagine rises and peaks every ninety minutes. After the peak, brain function declines for a time and then rises to another peak.

So our days are composed of these ninety-minute peaks of activity. If we could learn our brain cycle, we could plan our day to take advantage of these peak periods and to rest during the periods of decline. Instead of working solid for eight hours, we would work for thirty to forty-five minutes at a time and then take a break until we were through the low point of the cycle.

---

come today is the computer, which does not really resemble the human brain at all. However, by using the computer, we can simulate a brain or, as Rodolfo Llinás and András Pellionisz of New York University Medical Center and Donald Perkel of Stanford have done, a portion of the brain. These three researchers, after eight years of work, have successfully programmed a computer to imitate the action of the human cerebellum.

How does one build a brain in a computer? By feeding into the machine the dimension and number of neurons in the cerebellum and then ordering the computer to connect those simulated cells. Llinás and Pellionisz made an assumption that the genetic material within the neuron is not large enough to direct nerve cells to link up with specific other nerve cells. Rather, each neuron's axon and dendrites grow out at random until they hit other groups of cells. To test their artificial cerebellum, the scientists hooked their computer up to a mechanical arm. Then they ordered the computer to write out the word "OK." First, the computer ran its command to the arm through the created cerebellum. The "OK" was written smoothly in clear, round letters. Next, the computer cut the cerebellum out of the command circuit. The arm wavered, and the word "OK" was written in jerky, wavy letters, very much as though by a person suffering from a damaged cerebellum.

Since the simulated cerebellum worked and since it was based on randomly connected neurons, Llinás and Pellionisz have some evidence for believing the brain works through random connections. Thus, what neurons connect with what other neurons seems to be unimportant to the brain. The researchers feel that what is important in the neural working of the brain is the pattern formed by the simultaneous firing of many neurons. If we wished to have a complete understanding of a single event in history, such as the beginning of the Revolutionary War, we would read many different accounts by not just American colonists, but also by British and French writers. The brain, likewise, builds up an image or understands a message by taking the accounts of several thousand different neurons, correlating them, and arriving at a unified picture.

And what does the brain use to create this image? According to Llinás and Pellionisz, we can see the brain as similar to a large multi-dimensional graph. We are familiar with conventional graphs with an axis x, running left and right, and a second axis y, running up and down. We can also add a third axis z that runs back and forward, so that we can draw three-dimensional graphs. We can continue adding axes to represent all the other theoretical dimensions that mathematicians and physicists have postulated. Using this model, we assume that each neuron is one of these axes, x,y,z, etc. With a regular graph, we would place a point on an axis by measuring a number of units, inches, meters, whatever. For our brain model, the distance along the axis depends upon the number of times a neuron fires.

You are looking at a square, red plastic block. The picture of the block is transmitted to your mind through the simultaneous firing of thousands of neurons. On the graph that is your mind, a neuron fires telling your brain that the block is square. Another does the same for the color red. Another for plastic. The degree of squareness, redness, and plasticness are also indicated. So, a single point is determined on the brain graph that stands for only the image of this square, red plastic block. A smaller, redder plastic block would be at a different point.

We still have much to learn about the functioning of our brains. Yet already we are beginning to see not only what our brains do, but how they do it. We are developing ways of using this knowledge to help ourselves to be more the masters of our behavior than its slaves. As András Pellionisz answers when asked if the understanding of the brain's operation is beyond our comprehension, "Of course not. Not at all."

VIDEOGAMING YOUR WAY BACK TO HEALTH

Recently, several communities have attempted to impose regulations upon minors playing videogames. Concerned parents and psychologists feel that some children are spending too much time playing such games and not learning to interact with other children.

Videogames, however, have found a champion in at least one quarter. Psychologist William J. Lynch of the Veterans Medical Center of Palo Alto, California has been using games such as Breakout, Pong, and Air-Sea Battle to help victims of brain damage, stroke, and senile dementia to recover some of their speech and coordination. The demands of these videogames hone these abilities. One patient, whose left hemisphere had been injured, played Breakout for a month and went from twenty hits to fifty. He was soon able to leave the hospital and to find a job.

Renee Okoye and Tony Hollander, working with children having learning disabilities, successfully used galactic video war games. The children improved their hand-eye coordination as well as their spatial visualization.

Perhaps, in the future, Asteroids will be a permanent feature in hospitals and schools.

4

Looking from Within: The Perceiving Brain

Although Roy is not familiar with the room, he has no difficulty getting around in it. Hotel rooms are a part of an industrial consultant's life, and Roy spends much of his year in such rooms. He slips the last few papers into his briefcase. Then, after latching the case, he feels around on the bed for his coat. Finding it, he pulls it on, being careful not to disconnect accidently the wire leads from his glasses and his bone conductor earphone. The coat has been tailored to hide the slight thickness of the tactile stimulator vest and the flat bulge of the microcomputer strapped to his back. Without this equipment, Roy is blind.

Ready to go, Roy turns his head in the direction of the bedside table that holds the telephone. The small TV camera mounted to the side of his glasses transmits the images of phone and table to the computer. Through his earphone, the computer's voice tells Roy, "Table. Phone. Straight ahead." Roy walks ahead, stopping when the computer says, "Stop." He then picks up the receiver and calls the desk, asking for a cab. Then, picking up his briefcase, Roy leaves the room. Walking to the elevator, he avoids the maid's cart. The computer tells him, "Object. Four feet distant. Angle right."

Taking the elevator to the ground floor, Roy walks through the lobby, moving to the right, to the left, stepping up or down according to the instructions flowing out of his computer backpack. He walks out through the sliding glass doors just as his cab pulls up. The driver notices the headband Roy is wearing.

"You an Indian or something?"

"No. It's part of my substitute vision system," Roy says. He explains the system, ending with, "And the headband contains stimulators that tap me in case I don't catch the computer direction. One tap for right. Two for left. And so on."

The cab lets Roy off at the electronics firm that he is advising about assembly procedures. Since he was here the previous day, he does not have to ask directions to the fifth floor conference room. His computer remembers the route and steers him directly to it.

Waiting for him are three engineers. His computer tells him who is standing where. Roy shakes hands all around, addressing each by name. The computer also passes on its analysis of the engineers' facial expressions. They are all happy to see Roy and look eager to get down to work. Some new reports have just come in, and Roy needs to study them before the conference can continue. So, he pulls out of his coat pocket his Reader, a small, rectangular device with a series of photoelectric cells on one face and a number of small wires on the opposite. When Roy passes the Reader across a line of writing, he feels the wires vibrating against his fingers. The vibrations represent the images of letters picked up by the photoelectric cell. Roy's training has taught him to read the differences in the vibrations. With his Reader, he is able to read some eighty words a minute. Roy may be physically blind, but his equipment allows him to function almost as though he were not.

Roy, of course, is not real, nor can the blind yet operate this naturally. Still, we are close. The tactile stimulator, the computer voice direction, and the Reader have their prototypes today, and research on these and other aids to the blind are continuing at such places as the Smith-Kettlewell Institute of Visual Science and the National Eye Institute. The work in this area is so rapid that Roy's equipment, the common use of which still lies in the future, may seem crude and primitive within the next ten years.

The Multiple Senses

Most of us feel that vision is the most important of our senses. And indeed, we are probably more conscious of what we see than what we hear, smell, taste, or feel. We worry more about problems with our eyes than we do with problems with our other senses, except to some extent for our hearing. However, even deafness does not provoke the fear that blindness does. Thus, we should not be surprised that most of the research on our five senses has been confined to the study of sight: how the eyes work, how the vision centers of the brain operate, and what can be done for poor eyesight and blindness.

Yet vision is only a single part of our perception of our world. Our other senses are also important in building up that composite picture of the world that acts upon us through our perception. Our brain perceives our surroundings not only through the images seen by the eyes, but also through sounds heard by the ears, odors smelled by the nose, tastes on the tongue, and touch and pressure on the skin.

Reception of four of these senses is confined to specific organs, the eyes, the ears, the nose, and the tongue. The fifth, touch, however, has receptors scattered over the entire surface of the skin. Receptors are nerve endings that respond to a particular sensation. Those on the skin to touch, in the eye to light, in the ear to sound, and so on. Although, in using the term touch, we are thinking of being able to feel something, we also tend to use the word rather loosely. In addition to the receptors of touch, the skin also has receptors for heat, cold, and pressure. So, when we speak of the sense of touch, we are actually speaking or four different senses. The traditional idea of five senses is wrong. In actuality, we have at least eight.

Sense receptors are specific. A receptor of touch reports to the brain only touch. Ones for heat report only heat, and ones for cold, only cold. However, as we shall see, once these signals reach the brain, they can be reinterpreted. Such reinterpretation is the basis for the *sensory substitution* involved in the research that leads to the stimulator-computer vision system of our consultant Roy.

The receptor sites for touch, pressure, heat, and cold are scattered over the surface of the body, but their dispersal is not uniform. If we made a map of the world's population, we would see large concentrations of people around large cities such as New York, London, Tokyo and in long-settled land such as Europe and the eastern United States. Large portions of our map, however, would show little or no population. Just as with a map of the world's population, a map of the receptor sites on the human skin would show large clumps of such sites at certain points. Between these groups, we would see only a relatively few sites. Thus, our fingertips have many touch receptors, while our backs have only a few. We would expect this difference since, to make the best manipulative use of our fingers, we need them to be sensitive to touch. And sensitive they are; the fingertips can tell the difference between two touches only one-tenth of an inch apart, while two such touches have to be over three inches apart on the back.

In addition to receptors for touch, pressure, heat, and cold, our skins also have receptors for pain. In one sense, pain receptors are related to the other four since too great a pressure, such as hitting an arm against a doorjamb, or too much heat, such as touching a hot stove, causes pain. The pain receptors take over when the sensations

THE OTHER SENSES

We take it for granted that we have five senses. But why only five? Other animals have senses beyond the conventional sight, sound, touch, smell, and taste, so why not humans as well?

Pit vipers, snakes such as the rattlesnake and the copperhead, have a small hole between the nostrils and eye, the pit, which detects differences in temperature. A rattlesnake can sense a one-thousandth degree difference in temperature, which allows it and other pit vipers to find warmblooded prey easily.

Most birds are able to sense the differences in the position of the sun, moon, and stars so that they can navigate large distances with great accuracy. Seabirds can easily and reliably find isolated islands that human pilots with sophisticated instrumentation sometimes have problems locating.

Some snails can even detect changes in the earth's magnetic field due to fluctuations in the ionosphere.

And what about humans? Most of us have some sort of time sense. Without looking at a clock, we can generally tell roughly how much time has passed. Also, we can learn to beat our alarm clocks by setting our inner timer to wake us after a certain number of hours.

Also, like other species, we are sensitive to changes in seasons. With birds and other animals, the angle of the sun as well as the intensity of the sunlight tells them that spring has arrived and that it is time for breeding. Anyone who has had "spring fever" knows that we also respond to the arrival of spring.

We are perhaps too complacent about our assumptions concerning our senses. A little bit of thought shows that we have more senses than is generally believed.

---

involved become too large for the other receptors, which means injury and danger for us. Although we generally think of these five senses, touch, pressure, heat, cold, and pain, as associated with our skin, we realize on reflection they are also found inside our bodies as well. Anyone who has torn a muscle knows the sensation of internal pain,

and certainly hot foods and cold liquids can be felt in our mouths, if
they are hot and cold enough. Still, except for pain, these five are felt
most strongly and most consistently through the receptors in our
skins.

As you sit reading this book, are you conscious of your clothing or
the chair against your body? Probably, you are now that your attention has been attracted to clothing and chairs. Before, however,
unless the chair is uncomfortable and unless your clothes are too
tight, you were not conscious of either. Yet both the senses of touch
and pressure are involved when anything touches or presses on your
skin, and certainly clothing and sitting in a chair involve both.

Are the senses of touch and pressure unreliable? No. Unless the
stimulus constantly changes, receptors of touch, pressure, heat, and
cold will stop reacting. If they did not do so, they would be sending the
brain a constant stream of needless information. Instead, after the
brain has been informed of these sensations, it is only informed again
if the receptors detect a change. If a friend calls and says he is on his
way over, he does not have to keep calling until he arrives. Only if he
is going to be unexpectedly late or is unable to make it will he call
again.

Pain receptors, however, do not cut off as do those of touch,
pressure, heat, and cold. Since pain is a signal of something wrong
with the body, it continues until the problem is corrected so that the
brain will not ignore or forget the injury.

The more specialized receptors for sight, sound, taste, and smell
also have a cutoff for continuous stimuli. Anyone who has ever lived
near a busy street knows that the sounds of the traffic soon cease to be
a bother.

In Chapter 1, we saw how neurons operate. Acetylcholine from
the axon of one nerve cell stimulates the dendrites of the next cell,
causing sodium ions to enter the cell and potassium ions to leave. The
resulting flow produces an electrical difference and an electrical
signal that moves down the neuron. The initial trigger for all of these
processes is the *stimulation* of a receptor. Thus, if you place an ice
cube in the palm of your hand, receptors of touch, pressure, and cold
are activated. The neurons composing the nerve fibers leading from
each set of receptors produce acetylcholine, go through the ion exchange, and pass the signal from neuron to neuron along the entire
length of the fiber up through the brain stem and to the appropriate
regions of the cerebrum. To get into the cerebrum, all of these impulses must pass through the thalamus, which is important, as we
shall see, in sensory substitution. Only information from the nose

goes directly to the cerebrum without moving through the brain stem and thalamus.

All our senses operate the same way. A receptor, which will only react to a specific stimulus, gives rise to a signal that is converted into information in the cerebrum. Just as NASA learned about Jupiter and Saturn through information processes by the instruments on Voyager I and II, we learn about our world through information fed to our brains. Thus, we do not perceive anything directly but rather secondarily in our brains. When we run our thumb across an unsanded board, the roughness is sensed not in our fingertips, but in our cerebrum.

Tracking Sight

But what happens to the nerve signal once it reaches the cerebrum? What does the brain actually do with signals denoting touch in the sensory region, sound in the auditory, or sight in the visual? Unfortunately, researchers are only just beginning to study the mechanisms by which the brain converts this sense information into a complete picture of the outside world. Indeed, except for an intensive program by Drs. David Hubel and Torsten Wiesel of the Harvard Medical School investigating the vision center of the cerebrum, little work has been done in this area. However, Hubel and Wiesel's work, for which they recently shared the Nobel Prize in Medicine, is beginning to tell us a great deal about how we "see," not how the eye works, but how the brain creates coherent visual images out of electrical impulses.

Vision

Of our sense organs, the eyes fascinate us most. Poets and writers have called them the "windows to the soul." Popular folk wisdom claims that a person's eyes will reveal his or her intentions. And the eyes are unique. Information from the right-hand sense receptors are fed to the left brain, while data from the left-hand receptors go to the right brain. With the eyes, however, only half of the input in the right eye goes to the left brain; the remainder goes to the right brain. And

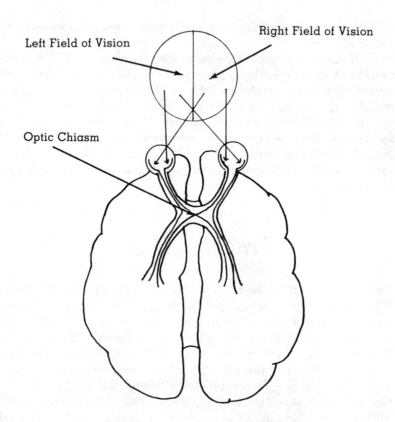

Left Field of Vision   Right Field of Vision

Optic Chiasm

Figure 1.   The optic chiasm, where the optic nerves cross over. Despite each eye taking in portions of both left and right fields of vision, all of the right field of vision goes to the left brain and all of the left field of vision goes to the right brain.

so it is with the left eye: half is fed to the right brain and half to the left (see Figure 1).

The optic nerves from the left and right eye cross in an X-shaped structure, the optic chiasm. Here the nerve fibers from the right half of the left eye and right half of the right eye go to the right brain. The fibers from the left half of the left eye and the left half of the right eye go to the left brain. So, only part of the information from each eye is fed to the opposite cerebral hemisphere. Why is this crossover only partial in the eye whereas it is complete with the other sense organs? Unlike many animals, such as rabbits whose eyes are set on the side of the head, ours are set in the front. The left eye of a rabbit will see everything on the left and the right eye everything on the right.

Thus, the rabbit's left eye passes its input to the right brain and its right eye to the left brain. Our front-mounted eyes, however, can only see half of the field of vision in front of them. The left eye can see half of the left field of vision and the right eye half of the right field of vision. In order for both fields of vision to be completely observed by our eyes, half of each eye must take in sight from the opposite field of vision.

Once this is done, all of the information from the right field of vision goes to the left brain and all of the input from the left field to the right brain. The crossover is necessary, therefore, to keep the distinction between right and left brain input.

The Gift of Sight?

Helen Keller, blind from birth, speculated on the magnificence of sight and what it would be like to see after a lifetime of blindness. In 1958, a fifty-two-year-old British man, blind since he was ten months old, underwent surgery which restored his sight. What should have been a miracle turned into a tragedy. Within the year, this outgoing, self-reliant man was dead after becoming a virtual recluse and undergoing a deep depression. What went wrong?

At first, this patient was excited by the world his new sense opened up to him. Quickly, however, his excitement waned, and disappointment began dominating his reactions. Although awed by the colors of a sunset, this man found its beauty so fleeting and in such stark contrast to the average sights of the day that he could not reconcile himself to what he considered everyday drabness. Worse than this disappointment was his inability to feel that what he saw had any meaning or reality to him. Conditioned by a half century of sensing his world only through touch and sound, he could not look at a person or thing and comprehend what he was seeing. Once, when shown a cutting lathe, he was unable to understand its operation by looking at it. When, however, he closed his eyes and began feeling the lathe, he immediately grasped its purpose.

Depression soon followed from this man's constant disappointment in the visual world and in his consistent inability to understand that world. While he was blind, he showed no hesitation about walking out into heavy traffic, confident in his ability to use sound and touch to get across the street. With sight, he became confused and disordered, unable to find that old confidence.

Does this case mean that work toward eliminating blindness should stop? No, but it does show that problems exist in correcting what we traditionally view as handicaps. What to us may be a handicap may not be to someone else. In determining how best to help someone, doctors in the future are going to have to be very careful. Also, human perception is far more complex and versatile than we have given it credit for being in the past. The man whose sight was restored after nearly a lifetime of blindness was unable to adjust to his new perception of the world. Does this mean that we are so tightly bound to our perception of our world that any change in what our senses perceive will leave us floundering helplessly? In some cases, yes, but experiments have shown that the brain can adjust to new sensory information.

Drs. R. Held and A. Hein placed newborn kittens into a completely dark room for several months. Then they brought them out into the light. Some kittens were allowed to walk around the room, while others were placed in baskets dragged by the free kittens. The kittens in the first group eventually learned to see, but the others did not.

In 1897, a University of California psychologist, G.M. Stratton, manufactured and wore a pair of goggles whose lenses made the world appear upside down and reversed from side to side. At first, Stratton felt he had stumbled into a dream world. Nothing seemed real, and he had difficulty moving around. After a few days, however, of constantly wearing the goggles and forcing himself to carry on his normal activities, the world appeared perfectly normal again. When he finally took the goggles off, several days of readjustment were needed because the normal world now looked odd.

In a more recent experiment, subjects wore glasses with different colored lenses. The results were the same. Participants needed several days to adjust, but once adjusted, the world appeared perfectly normal. When they removed their glasses, the world returned to normal in several days.

The ability to adjust rests with the active exploration of the person's world. Only the kittens that walked around learned to see; and only when the human subjects began to move around did they adjust. During such exploration, the other senses are apparently coordinated with the new, changed sense, leading to the ability to handle the new perception. That coordination enables the brain to find meaning in this new information.

Medieval thinkers often thought that the brain contained a very tiny man who, sitting in the middle of the brain, took in all the information from the various senses and passed that collected information onto the person. Such an idea did not survive even the dissection of a single brain. Nor would it survive an examination of an autoradiograph of the primary vision center of the brain.

What would our little man see? He would see radioactively labeled swirls much like the patterns in a chocolate marble cake. He would make little sense out of this activity, yet to the brain, the

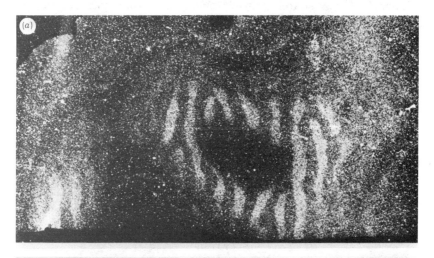

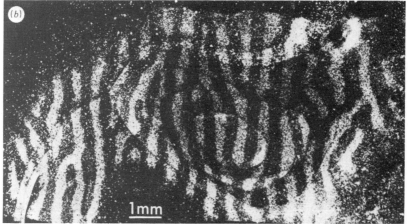

Autoradiograph of the cross section of the primary visual cortex, showing the swirling pattern (the white lines) of the ocular dominance columns. (1 mm = 0.04 inch) (Reprinted, with permission, from David H. Hubel, Harvey Lectures: Effects of Deprivation on the Visual Cortex of Cat and Monkey © *1978 by Academic Press)*

patterns are of immense significance. These labeled swirls are cross sections of the *ocular dominance columns,* one of the findings from Hubel and Wiesel's work. The two researchers began their study some twenty years ago, and, by inserting microelectrodes into selected cells in the retina of the eye and along the optic nerve, they traced visual signals back to a group of cells called the *lateral geniculate body* and from them to the *primary visual cortex* or center (see Figure 2). This research was done using macaque monkeys but, as Hubel observes, "Neural tissue and chemistry in all species is basically the same."

The *retina,* which is in the back of our eyes, holds the receptors for light. These receptor cells have two parts: a circular center and a circular border. A spot of light falling on the center of these receptors will cause it to send a signal along the optic nerve. If that spot falls onto the border, no signal will be sent or the outgoing signals will be halted. Each of these cells is very sensitive to position and will only react to images at a specific point in an animal's field of vision.

When the receptors of the retina are stimulated, they send an impulse along the optic nerve to the *lateral geniculate bodies.* Everything we see to the right goes to the left geniculate body, while

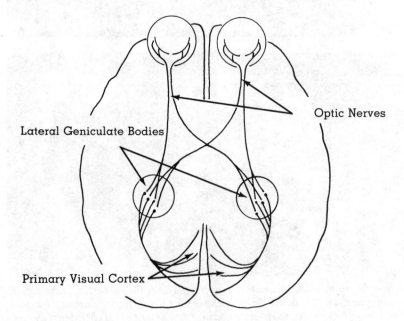

Figure 2.   The path of vision from the eyes down the optic nerves to the lateral geniculate bodies and finally to the primary visual cortex.

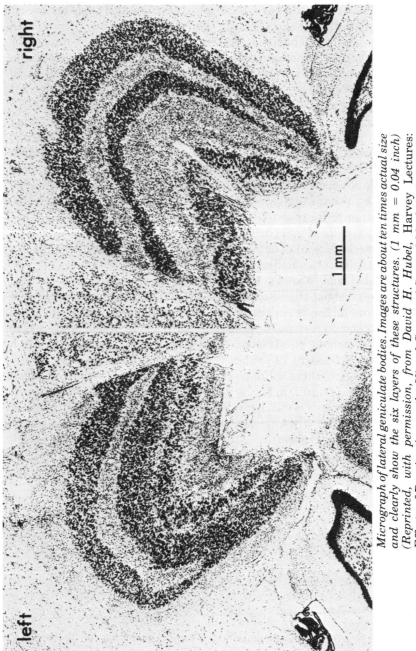

Micrograph of lateral geniculate bodies. Images are about ten times actual size and clearly show the six layers of these structures. (1 mm = 0.04 inch) (Reprinted, with permission, from David H. Hubel, Harvey Lectures: Effects of Deprivation on the Visual Cortex of Cat and Monkey © 1978 by Academic Press)

everything we see from the left goes to the right body. To understand how this is done, see page 94. Each geniculate body has six layers (see Figure 3).

The geniculate bodies act as relay stations. If they have any other functions, those functions are not yet known. Perhaps, however, the nerve impulses get a boost from these geniculate bodies since the trip from the retina to the primary visual center is a long one. The visual cortex is located, of course, at the back of the cerebrum.

The primary visual cortex has at least two ways of processing signals from both eyes. The ocular dominance columns (see Figure 4) get information from both eyes. These columns put that information together. The second set of columns, the orientation columns, deal with the position of an object in a field of vision. Thus some of the cells in these columns activate when we see something to the far right, while other cells are stimulated by objects in other places, such as the far left. Simple visual cortex cells respond differently from complex cells (see Figure 5). The orientation columns are more chaotically arranged than the ocular dominance columns.

Hubel and Wiesel's work has produced some of the first real knowledge about the relationship between functioning in an area of the brain and the brain's structure. The presence of columns in other areas of the cerebrum, those controlling hearing, touch, and speech, for example, have also been detected. Columns in the auditory region alternate processing of sounds from the right and left ears. In the sensory region, these columns respond to bending hairs, direct touch on the skin, pressure in joints, and so on. The function of the columns in the speech area is still not understood. Hubel and Wiesel are quick to point out that, although the primary visual cortex now is the most thoroughly mapped region of the brain, the mapping has only begun.

Figure 3. Artist's representation of a lateral geniculate body and its six layers.

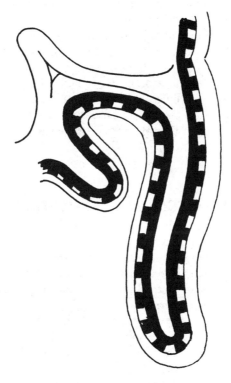

Figure 4.   Cross section of the ocular dominance column of the primary visual cortex. The white squares represent the columns that process information from either right or left eye.

Figure 5.   Difference between response for simple visual cortex cell (left) and complex cell (right). For the simple cell, the line must be at an exact angle in an exact position. For the complex cell, the line must be at an exact angle, but it can be in any position.

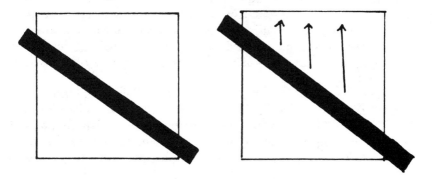

The two researchers are now looking for more columns, columns for depth perception and color vision.

Also, both Hubel and Wiesel are aware that the primary visual cortex is only the beginning of the processing of visual signals by the cerebrum. The information is fed from this region to many others where much of the correlation between sight and the other senses is carried out. Twenty years of work has produced a great deal of information about how our brains perceive our world, but that twenty years is only the beginning of our full understanding of such perception.

Overcoming Damage

While some researchers are investigating how the brain deals with the data from the various senses, others are developing ways to deal with a breakdown in those senses. Blindness, deafness, and speech impairment can arise from damage to specific areas of the brain, injury or destruction of nerves, or defects in sense organs or receptors. Thus a soldier who receives a piece of shrapnel in the rear of the cerebrum, where the visual cortex is located, will probably live, but he will be blind. If the right acoustic nerve should die, then a person will be deaf in his or her right ear. A detached retina, which contains the sight receptors, will result in blindness.

Most of the research on blindness and deafness concentrates on people having problems with eyes or ears and with optic or acoustic nerves. Retraining the brain to shift the functions from damaged to healthy regions has, as we have seen, not been particularly successful. The actual brain regions still exist intact and can still operate, but they are cut off from needed sensory information. The problem, therefore, is how to resupply the brain. The best solution obviously would be to feed data directly into the visual, auditory, or sensory cortex. We know that you can implant electrodes and stimulate parts of the brain, so why not construct an array of microelectrodes, insert them into the visual cortex of a blind person, hook the electrodes up to a camera, and await results?

Indeed, a British scientist, Dr. G.S. Brindley, in the late 1960's implanted eighty electrodes into a blind patient. His purpose was to see if he could activate the visual cortex at all, which he did, and whether prolonged presence of the electrodes as well as electrical stimulation of the brain would harm the patient. Brindley discovered

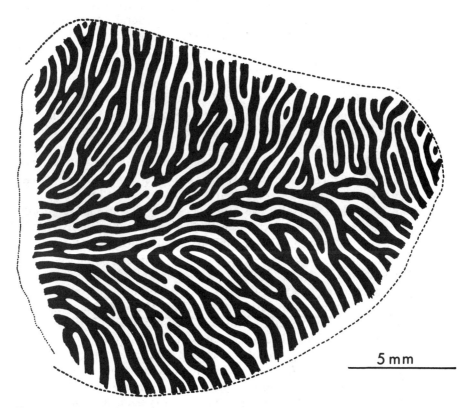

Representation of the entire cross section of the right primary visual cortex, showing the autoradiograph white swirls of the ocular dominance columns. (5 mm = 0.2 inch) (Reprinted, with permission, from David H. Hubel, Harvey Lectures: Effects of Deprivation on the Visual Cortex of Cat and Monkey © 1978 by Academic Press)

that brief periods of stimulation were not harmful and that patients could tolerate the electrodes for up to five years. In 1972 Brindley was able to insert electrodes into the visual cortex of a patient blind for over thirty years. This person was eventually able to recognize Braille letters because of the electrical stimulation of the electrodes.

Unfortunately, implantation of even microelectrodes presents several problems, which at present appear to be insolvable. First, microelectrodes are treated by the brain as foreign invaders, and consequently scar tissue builds up around them, isolating them from the neural tissue. Second, even microelectrodes are too large for the numbers of electrodes that would need to be inserted into a specific region of the brain to activate it fully: they crowd each other out. Finally, microelectrodes can only function at a certain speed, nowhere near the rate of firing of neurons, so microelectrodes will be inactive too much of the time, leaving the brain cut off during those periods.

Whether these problems with implanted electrodes can be overcome is a matter for the future. At present, however, work is progressing rapidly on various prostheses, particularly for the blind. Such aids are already common for the partially handicapped: hearing aids for the hard-of-hearing and multilensed glasses for those with extremely poor eyesight. The cane is a prosthetic device for the blind. New technologies, however, have produced new aids. Now we have the laser cane. The laser cane throws out three laser beams, two at head level, one at foot level. When the top two beams hit something, they buzz, thus warning the blind person. The bottom beam only buzzes when it does not encounter an object so that the person will not fall into open manholes or stumble over curbs or down stairs.

The *Optacon*, developed at Stanford University in the early 1970's, is one of the reading devices for the blind. The old Braille system, although useful, is limited since the blind do not have access to materials until translated into braille. The Optacon, however, reads any regularly printed material. Weighing about eight pounds, this device has a small camera that registers the image of a letter. This image then is tapped out onto the tip of the user's finger through an array of 144 rods. Although requiring practice to use, the Optacon allows the blind to read up to eighty words a minute. An attachment can allow a blind typist to read and correct typed copy while still in the typewriter.

Other prostheses appearing on the market now are new readers: one looks like a large flashlight and, through vibrations to the user's hand, signals the letters being scanned. Infra-red and sonar detectors, both hand-held and mounted into the frames of glasses, are being used to replace canes and seeing-eye dogs. Talking signs are being installed in some cities and buildings.

Substituting the Senses

Even without mechanical aids, the brain itself often provides help to the blind. The increased sensitivity among the blind to sound, smell, touch is almost a cliché for us, but this enhancement of senses certainly exists. The Air Force uses blind workers to check by feel the fan blades of jet fighter engines: their touch is more reliable than most

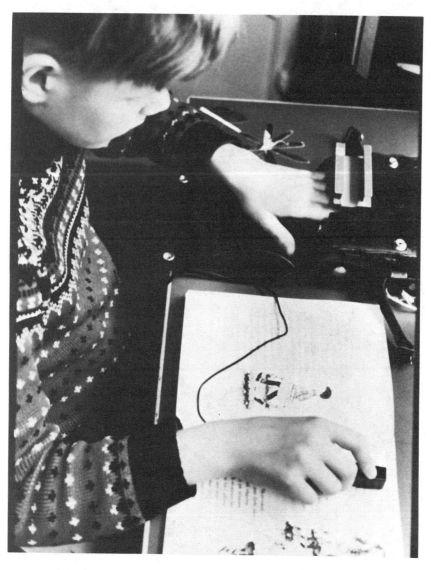

Optacon reader for the blind. To the right is the photocell unit. Inside can be seen where the index finger is placed. (Courtesy Telesensory Systems, Inc.)

Man wearing TVSS unit. (Courtesy Carter Collins, Smith-Kettlewell Institute)

people's eyesight. A movie like *If You Could Only See What I Hear* stresses over and over again the blind person's increased sensitivity.

Traditionally, this enhancement was considered the brain's way of compensating for the loss of sight. But is this actually the case? Electrodes placed within the vision center of cats have shown that this region responds to more than just signals from the eyes. Close to half of the cells are stimulated by sound and touch. Thus, we can "see" with more than just our eyes. We can also see through touch. Touch can mimic vision. This is the basis for sensory substitution.

Taking this idea of one sense replacing another, Drs. Paul Bach-y-Rita and Carter C. Collins of the Smith-Kettlewell Institute of Visual Science in San Francisco constructed the first *Tactile Vision Substitution System (TVSS)* (see Figure 6). Originally, Bach-y-Rita and Collins's TVSS consisted of a grid with 400 skin stimulator points and a hand-held TV camera. The blind person would lean back in a chair with his back against the grid and then point the camera at objects such as a telephone, a cup, a toy Volkswagen, and so on. The image from the camera was fed into the skin stimulator grid, which would painlessly activate touch receptors on the subject's back. At first, the blind person saw nothing and could make no sense out of the stimulation of his skin. After ten or fifteen hours, however, he would forget that he was feeling the stimulator grid working and begin to perceive images.

Sound like magic? Not really. As Carter Collins observes, "The process is familiar to most of us who played a children's game. Somebody would write a letter on your back or on your palm. You would know almost immediately what the letter was.

"This is the same principle we are making use of with perhaps a little more sophistication. The figures we draw on the skin, we derive from a television camera."

What these people perceived were black and white images, rather blocky and sketchy. Yet, they could make out what they saw. They were able through sensory substitution to "see" by touch.

A more advanced TVSS was quickly produced. The grid now had 1,024 stimulator points. These gave a more detailed image. The unit was now four pounds with the camera mounted on the frame of glasses. Unfortunately, the TVSS has certain drawbacks. First, although the recognition time for objects dropped from a few minutes to a few seconds, this time was not quick enough for going outside. "The world is much too complex," Collins says, "for the tactile system to be able to work well. There is too much noise, too much detail."

Another problem was discovered when TVSS subjects began

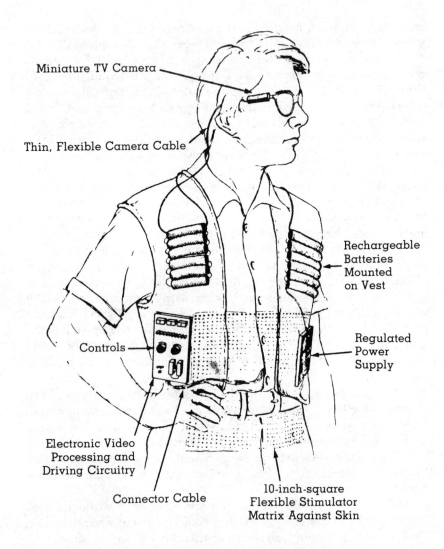

Miniature TV Camera

Thin, Flexible Camera Cable

Rechargeable
Batteries
Mounted
on Vest

Controls

Regulated
Power
Supply

Electronic Video
Processing and
Driving Circuitry

Connector Cable

10-inch-square
Flexible Stimulator
Matrix Against Skin

looking at friends and relatives. Excited at first at the prospect, each person showed, as he or she aimed the TVSS at other people, an increasing uneasiness and disappointment. Such problems had been previously encountered with people blind from birth who suddenly were given sight (see page 95). Those blind from birth experience the world through sound and touch. They do not feel that what they see is real. Additionally, their imaginations build their expectations to the point that no visual reality can satisfy them. With objects the problem for the previously blind is not so great. With people, how-

THE VISION OF CARTER COLLINS

Carter Collins is a researcher with the Smith-Kettlewell Institute of Visual Sciences, where he has been working for several years on TVSS, which enables the blind to "see."

Q: How have you modified your original TVSS concept over the years?

A: We tried two new approaches. The first was to simplify the world. We used an ultrasonic phased-array scanning sonar as the camera. This essentially made objects become single points, for which we could display range and distance.

With this apparatus people could navigate through the world quite well because of the simplicity of the display. If you saw two points, you would assume they were, say, two poles. Then you could arrange to move so they moved off to either side.

That worked out quite well. But it couldn't see a step down, so you might step off the edge of a curb and break your neck.

Q: And your other approach?

A: This seems to be the most promising. We took the output of a miniature TV camera and put it into a most sophisticated microcomputer, a Motorola 68000. We programmed the computer with artificial intelligence to the extent that the computer could recognize obstacles. We could then have it speak to the blind person in machine-generated speech, something like [in a monotone] "Pole. One O'Clock. Ten Feet."

Q: Then you don't plan to use the original TVSS concept anymore?

A: In a more limited sense, we will still use it. Such a system, however, will not be helpful in everyday mobility situations. The problem with using the skin in recognizing what an obstacle might be is that, although it can be learned, it is quite taxing. In fact it took so much effort that a blind person wasn't able to attend to a conversation. He had to spend all of his attentive power trying to determine what each obstacle or object might be.

So, we've taken that load off of him and put it onto the computer. Now he's quite free. Now all we use the skin for is to tell him where the object is located.

I use sixteen stimulators on a little belt, which we put around the forehead. It taps him in the direction of the obstacle. The number of taps tells him the distance. He can point right to it.

Q: You said that the more elaborate use of the skin for visual display still had some uses. What are those?

A: Education is one. A person with the TVSS can tell to some extent what's being scratched on the blackboard. He can also use it to look through a microscope, and it gives him a view he could not otherwise have of the microworld.

Employment is another area. We have had a blind technician go down to Hewlett-Packard and assemble microdiodes on the production line. We improved the apparatus and his training to the extent that he was able to do the job as well as the average worker on the line. So there is a considerable potential there.

Q: What do you see in the future? Electronic seeing-eye dogs?

A: The Japanese are working on just that, an electronic seeing eye dog. It's a little robot with camera and sensors that runs around on wheels. The user can essentially use the thing to sniff out a clear path.

The future, I believe, will lie in the use of computers with artificial intelligence to help the blind. I believe we can develop the technology so that a blind person will have a system that recognizes faces. We would program the microcomputer to recognize people and to recognize the expressions on their faces. From that, it would interpret emotion. Is the person pleased, angry, unhappy?

With this, and I believe it possible, a blind person should be able to interpret how his comments are coming across in a conversation.

Q: Do you think microelectrode implants will someday supplant your work?

A: I would hope that they would, but we haven't seen enough success yet. The idea is good, and I like the approach. But it is going to take another ten or twenty years of basic research in neurobiology to get around the problems of the microelectrode arrays making good contact, keeping good contact, and not doing damage to the cells that are there.

1,024-stimulator-point grid of TVSS system. (Courtesy Carter Collins, Smith-Kettlewell Institute)

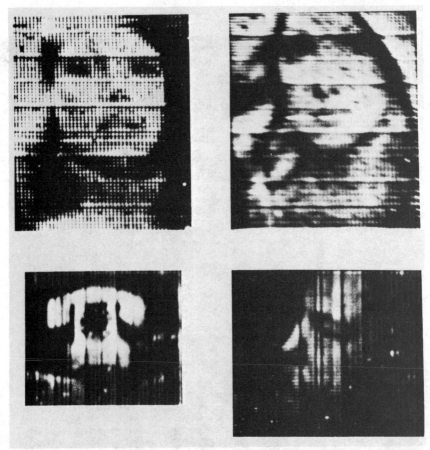

Approximation of images as seen by TVSS. (Courtesy Carter Collins, Smith-Kettlewell Institute)

ever, they find the problem of relating the visual image to the reality of their friend or relative too disturbing in many cases. They do not wish to see these people.

Therefore, although the TVSS is a significant step toward aiding the blind, it should not be seen as some kind of miracle cure for blindness. Blindness may not, indeed, be the handicap the sighted believe it to be. The blind often learn to cope successfully with their world. The addition of vision, not its absence, may be for them the handicap. So, instead of replacing vision, researchers may be helping many of the blind more by concentrating on more elaborate and efficient prostheses. Carter Collins has recently turned his efforts toward developing a camera-computer system which tells the blind person the position and distance of approaching objects and people.

Latest TVSS system, developed by Carter Collins. Camera feeds signals into computer, mounted on cart. Computer then tells blind person about approaching objects by voice and by taps from stimulator points contained in headband. (Courtesy Carter Collins, Smith-Kettlewell Institute)

Sensory substitution, however, has not been confined to aiding the blind. Tactile stimulator belts, according to Collins, now exist to convert touch into sound for the deaf. As our technology advances and our understanding of the workings of sensory substitution increases, tactile stimulator systems for both the blind and the deaf should become commonplace items.

However, even these systems may not be necessary in the future. Soon, microcircuits capable of doing the job of vision or sound receptors may be grafted directly onto the end of the optic or acoustic nerves. These artificial receptors will send light or sound impulses down the nerves to the brain, replacing the dead nerve ends.

Further away, advances in fiber optics may bring us the ability to replace a dead or dying optic nerve. Such filaments are replacing the old cables in phone systems because they can handle several thousand times the messages of the older wire. Before they can be used as nerve replacements, they would have to be able to carry many times even that number. But progress is ever-present.

We shall see.

5

Charting the Chemical Sea: The Chemistry of the Brain

So, Sperry and MacLean, Hubel and Wiesel have put us on the path to the brain's inner workings. But have we gone as far as we can? Do we now just have to keep monitoring the electrodes and microelectrodes to unravel all of the brain's secrets? Unfortunately, no.

The ultimate mystery of the brain lies within in its chemical makeup. The brain, like our entire body, is really nothing more than a complex series of chemical reactions. It is the relationships of these varying chemicals that must finally be discovered before we can say that we know how our brains work.

The discovery of the brain's chemistry was not especially rapid until the last decade. Studying chemical systems in any organism is not easy since there are so many of them and they are so difficult to separate from one another. The brain is no exception. However, within the last ten years, the brain's chemistry has begun to yield to the neurobiologists' laboratories.

The Brain's Own Opiates

The year, 1972, a mere decade ago, and a graduate student, Candace Pert, working under Solomon H. Snyder of Johns Hopkins Medical School, was attempting to isolate the brain receptors for the *opiates,* the active ingredients in opium, morphine, and heroin. Using radioactively tagged opiates, Pert discovered these sites were located in the thalamus and the limbic system, the emotional center of the brain (see Figure 1). The experiment was one of those rarities in scientific investigation. The results were perfectly clear and unquestionable. The opiates fit into the brain's receptors like a key into a lock, just as though they had been made for these sites.

And, it was this perfect fit that created a problem. If anything, the experiment had been too successful. The problem? The opiates in these drugs are from poppies that were originally native to the Middle East. How could the brain, anyone's brain, have receptors into which these chemicals from a flower could fit perfectly? Coincidence? After all, opium, although several thousand years old, is comparatively new when placed against the million or so years through which the human brain evolved. And morphine is only a century and a half old, heroin a century.

Coincidence it was, but not that the brain had developed specific receptors for this poppy's chemicals. Rather, this poppy had developed chemicals which were almost identical to chemicals naturally present in the human brain, indeed in all animal brains. These were the *enkephalins,* meaning substances within the brain, and the

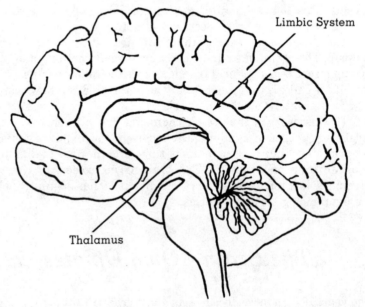

Figure 1. Location of opiate receptor sites in limbic system and thalamus.

ADDICTION

Why do heroin addicts have so much trouble kicking their habit? Even of those who manage, a large percentage sink back into the habit. Dr. Richard Restak proposes a possible explanation for the strength of heroin addiction. The heroin opiates grab onto the receptor sites that are normally occupied by endorphin. The brain knows through the buildup of unbound endorphin that these sites have chemicals in them, and so it tells the pituitary to stop manufacturing endorphin. The endorphin sites are filled, so there must be enough endorphin. Of course, the brain is wrong, but like a pilot flying on instruments, it must do as its readouts tell it.

Restak then proposes that, if the endorphin machinery stays shut down long enough, it may be difficult to restart. And the body needs endorphin. Thus, a long-term heroin addict may, when he goes cold turkey, be suffering not from a withdrawal of heroin, but from an endorphin shortage. Endorphin is not that readily available, so unless the pituitary starts reproducing endorphin, he may be forced back to the needle.

So, we may be looking at a cure for heroin addiction: not necessarily the injection of endorphin, but rather a technique for getting the machinery for endorphin production back in operation.

And how to do this? The signal for endorphin production is probably another neurotransmitter. Let future researchers isolate that transmitter. Then they can synthesize it, inject it into the reformed addict, and not only free him from his habit, but possibly avoid the whole unpleasant process of withdrawal.

---

endorphins, short for endogenous (internally produced) morphine. Structurally, enkephalins and endorphins are very similar to the opiates found in opium, morphine, and heroin.

How similar are these two chemicals to each other? And what is their relationship to each other? At first, neurochemists were not sure of the exact relationship between enkephalin and endorphin. Indeed, there were several endorphins, but the one that has been

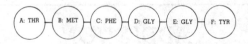

Figure 2.   *Amino acid sequence of enkephalin.*

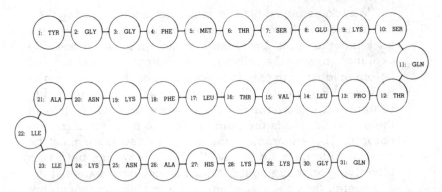

Figure 3.   Amino acid sequence of endorphin.

studied most thoroughly is *beta endorphin.* For simplicity's sake, we
will continue to call it endorphin. Both compounds are chains of
amino acids, the building blocks of proteins. Enkephalin, being a
much shorter amino acid chain, called a *peptide* (see Figure 2), is
perhaps contained within the endorphin peptide (see Figure 3). And,
as it turned out, part of the endorphin structure is like enkephalin.

It even began to make sense when the biochemists found that
enkephalins injected into the bloodstream immediately broke apart.
Endorphins, however, could circulate without problems. So, an initial
theory arose that the endorphins were a protective shell, much like
an egg's shell, surrounding the enkephalins. Thus, the larger chemical would defend and protect the smaller until it was needed.

An attractive theory, but it had one major flaw. Although enkephalin was found in many different parts of the brain (see Figure
4), endorphin was not. Endorphin was confined to a very small portion of the brain, the hypothalamus, just below the pain receptor sites
in the thalamus (see Figure 5). It didn't matter whether enkephalin
was contained within the endorphin or not. Since endorphin was only
found in one place and enkephalin in many, the endorphin could not
be carrying the enkephalin safely around. If it had, endorphin would
have been found in as many places as enkephalin.

But the answer was there. The neurochemists were not dealing

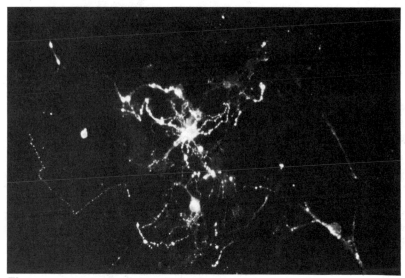

Fluorescent photograph of enkephalin-containing cells from mouse spinal column. (Courtesy Jeffery Barker, National Institute of Neurological and Communicative Disorders and Stroke)

with just two natural opiates. As Dr. Jeffery Barker of the National Institute of Neurological and Communicative Disorders and Stroke says, "Over the last couple of years, it has become quite clear that there are a whole family of opiod peptides, not just two. There are maybe up to ten."

One of these new peptides also contains enkephalin. And, as needed, it is found in the same areas of the brain as enkephalin. Indeed, even without knowing their distribution, neurochemists could see a chemical clue in these new peptides telling them that these were the protective shells for the enkephalin molecules. Unlike endorphin, the enkephalin in this new peptide is followed by two particular amino acids that are a common target for *enzymes* (see Figure 6). Enzymes are proteins or peptides that set off or accelerate chemical reactions in the body, and they are often involved in the breakup of other proteins or peptides. Thus, the presence of this enzymatic target in these new peptides adds that extra iota of evidence for these new peptides being enkephalin carriers. Now the biochemists could say how the enkephalin got free of its chemical shell so it could do its pain fighting duty.

The chemistry of the human body is extremely complex. Most of the chemical reactions that keep us alive and functioning are either not known or not completely understood. Thus, the amount of infor-

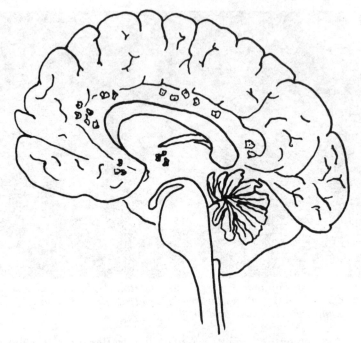

Figure 4.   Enkephalin is released at scattered points throughout the brain.

Figure 5.   Endorphin is released at a localized point in the brain.

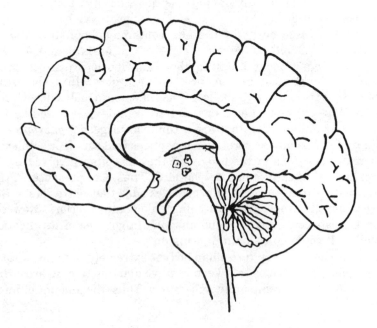

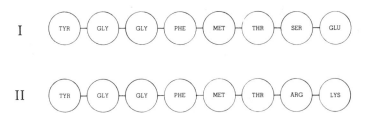

Figure 6. Comparison of enkephalin bonded into endorphin (I) and in actual
enkephalin carrier peptide (II). Notice that in II the enkephalin sequence is
followed by the amino acids lysine and arginine. These are the enzyme targets
that allow the release of enkephalin.

mation about endorphin and enkephalin chemistry is impressive. In
a mere ten years, the neurochemists have, from a single discovery,
revamped many of their ideas about the chemical systems of the
human body, particularly in relation to the nervous system.

Endorphin itself was quickly isolated as a product of the *pituitary gland,* a small body at the base of the cerebrum near the
hypothalamus and thalamus. Since endorphin bonds to the same
sites as the poppy opiates do, we would logically expect its production
site to be quite near the limbic system and the thalamus. But, if
enkephalin comes wrapped up in a larger package, so does endorphin.
This endorphin-containing peptide is manufactured in the pituitary,
and then is snipped apart by enzymes, much as you would a string
with a pair of scissors. Then, each of the parts speeds on its way to
perform its chemical duty.

Just what this peptide is and how large it is has come under
pretty constant re-evaluation over the last decade. The final consen-
sus is for a substance called *pro-opiomelanocortin,* a peptide that is
263 amino acids long. Compare that to the thirty-two amino acids in
endorphin and the six in enkephalin. However, it seems insignificant
when placed next to any protein, some of which may be several
thousand amino acids long.

More important for the understanding of how and what endorphin does was the discovery in 1977 that this long peptide contained
not only endorphin, but also *adrenocorticotrophic hormone, ACTH.*
ACTH stimulates the adrenal glands, which produce epinephrine
(adrenaline). Anyone who has ever been excited or frightened has
experienced the effects of adrenaline. Your breathing becomes heavy,
your heart races, and you feel a surge of energy. Adrenaline is also
produced when we are hurt. Thus, we see a chemical relationship

between endorphin and ACTH. The first alleviates pain. The second helps us cope with the stress of injury.

The Role of Enkephalin and Endorphin

Heroin, morphine, and opium are all effective painkillers. Therefore, the obvious conclusion about endorphin and enkephalin was that they, the body's own opiates, are part of the body's own pain control system. The neurochemists set out to prove this conjecture. And prove it they did.

Doctors at the University of California at San Francisco inserted electrodes into the brains, near the thalamus, of six patients who suffered from chronic, uninterrupted pain. By activating the electrodes, each patient could stop the pain. To be sure the effect was real, the physicians placed, without her knowledge, a dead battery in the electrode unit of one patient. She immediately complained that the pain would not stop. Replacing the bad battery stopped the pain.

Next, the doctors wanted to see if this electronic stimulation was producing endorphin. The researchers gave each patient an injection of *naloxone*. Naloxone binds to the same receptor sites in the thalamus as does endorphin. When naloxone is there, the endorphins can't get in. Since this blocking chemical does not activate these receptors, there is no pain relief. After the injections, the patients found that they could no longer electronically stop the pain. Only when the naloxone wore off, did the electrode stimulation once more have an effect.

Over the last several years, studies have been done on sufferers of migraine headaches. Chemical tests have shown that, just prior to the disappearance of the migraine, endorphin levels rise dramatically.

Endorphins may be the key to understanding some medically unexplainable treatments such as acupuncture. Prior to the endorphin revolution, doctors felt that the acupuncture needles were affecting neural centers found in various parts of the body. These centers were gates through which pain impulses had to pass. The insertion of the needle would close the gate, something like turning the crank of a castle drawbridge to shut it. Several experiments, however, seem to show that acupuncture needles stimulate the production of endorphin. These gates are actually locks holding the body's chemical pain relievers. The needles are the keys. A much more compelling explanation. At the Medical College of Virginia, David Mayer stimulated the nerves in volunteers' teeth. He then found that, by using acupuncture needles, he was able to control this pain. Then, like the San Francisco doctors, Mayer injected his volunteers with naloxone. Again, as in that earlier study, Mayer was unable to stop the pain with the needles until the naloxone was gone.

Acupuncture is not the only medical mystery to which endorphins may supply an answer. Like acupuncture, the placebo effect has puzzled doctors. For years, no one had an explanation how *placebos,* pills or injections containing no actual medicine, work. Placebos should do no harm, but neither should they do any good. Yet they often decrease or eliminate pain. Patients often call for more medicine, particularly pain killers. Since increased doses of any drug can be harmful, doctors often prescribe placebos. For them to work, the patient, however, must not know what he is getting. Obviously, when placebos work, the patient's mind convinces itself that it is feeling relief from pain. But, what is even more astounding is an actual chemical response to the placebos. Chemically, the body shows signs of the prescribed medicine at work.

One proposal to account for the effect of placebos is endorphin and enkephalin production. Tests of placebos, much like early endorphin tests at San Francisco and Virginia, showed that placebos do not work at all when patients are given naloxone, the endorphin block. When naloxone was not administered or when it wore off, about one-third of the patients tested reported that the placebos worked.

Wouldn't it be wonderful if we could persuade our bodies to produce endorphins whenever we needed them? It would, but of course, things are never that simple. Indeed, the question why people suffer from chronic pain has never really been answered. Pain is a signal of something wrong, but when it itself interferes with our health, becomes a disabling disorder, why doesn't the body begin producing endorphin and enkephalin and erase the pain?

"I don't know the answer to that one," answers one NIH researcher. "A very difficult question and a very subtle one. Why does the nervous system go awry? Why is there chronic pain? Why is there epilepsy? Why is there depression? I'm sorry but I don't have the answer." Nor does anyone else. So, until we can learn those answers, we must content ourselves with finding ways of dealing with and correcting pain, epilepsy, depression, mental illness, and any number of other brain disorders. We will look at some of the methods for treating the sick brain in the next chapter.

Even More Chemicals? The Neurotransmitters and Neurohormones

But, when we begin to talk about these opiates' pain-controlling role in the body, we are only scratching the surface of their function. According to Barker, "Each may serve a different function, each may have a different receptor, and each receptor may have a different purpose."

What purposes? These are not entirely clear yet, but other chemicals have been linked with nerve transmission, Enough of them so that neurochemists can echo the words of Dr. J. Eric Holmes, who observes, "There are a lot more transmitter-receptor systems than most of us would have suspected as recently as ten years ago. Then, we thought that, if you discussed norepinephrine and acetylcholine, you had pretty well discussed all the transmitters. It looks now like there must be twenty or thirty different transmitters in the brain."

In Chapter 1, we saw how nerve impulses were shot from neuron to neuron by the release of acetylcholine. Acetylcholine, however, is not the only chemical capable of bridging the synapse and activating adjacent neurons. The current estimate of such is between thirty and fifty, of which about forty have been studied to date. Some neurochemists even set the ultimate number at over 200.

Yet, for all these numbers, very few of the suspected chemicals have actually been classified as *neurotransmitters* (the name for such substances)—less than a dozen. Identifying these neurotransmitters is not easy. Nor is it always a simple matter deciding what they do, particularly since many seem to have more than one function. To be a neurotransmitter, a chemical must be found in the right neurons. If it is supposed to work on neurons in the hypothalamus, it better not be found in the visual cortex. It must be found at the end of the axon of a nerve cell, not far from the next cell's dendrite. There must be some way, a transport mechanism, for the transmitter to get from where it is made to the axon end. A synthetic of this suspected transmitter must be able to activate the proper neurons. Further, a second chemical must be found. This one breaks up the transmitter, just as cholinesterase breaks up acetylcholine, to keep it from continuing to work on the neuron. Finally, the target, the receptor, for this transmitter must be found.

One of the difficulties in studying these chemicals is, as Alan

TOO MUCH OF A GOOD THING

If we had really high endorphin levels, pain might be a thing of the past. But are you sure? Certainly pain is unpleasant, and we do our best to avoid it, yet it serves a purpose. Pain warns us when something is wrong. Indeed, it keeps us from inadvertently hurting ourselves.

Some people seem to be born with such high levels of endorphin that they can feel no pain. One such person was the daughter of a Canadian doctor. She was impervious to pain her whole life, but that life was filled with injury and an early death at twenty-nine from infections resulting from unnoticed cuts. At the age of two, she chewed the tip of her tongue into a pulp because she could feel no pain. A year later, while watching other children play, she kneeled on a radiator so hot she developed third-degree burns. As a teenager, her party trick was to dislocate each shoulder and then shrug them back into place.

When she died, the autopsy of her body revealed nothing unusual, but the discovery of endorphin was still in the future. Would a chemical analysis of her blood have revealed astonishing levels of endorphin? Probably.

There definitely is too much of a good thing.

Gevins remarks, "measuring the chemistry of a living brain. No one knows how to do that really. Several labs have been talking about radioactively labeling neurotransmitters and picking up their emissions with a PETT scanner. But I don't know of anyone who has actually done that yet." So the researchers must work with animals and very cautiously with human beings. The progress may not be as rapid as hoped for, but it has come along at quite a pace since Candace Pert labeled those opiate sites in 1972.

Also, this research has shaken up traditional ideas about the chemical coordination of brain activity. In the past, two chemical systems, each distinct from the other, were the coordinators of the working brain. They were the messengers that carried commands from the brain to the body, passed information back to the brain, and allowed the brain to talk with its various divisions. Thus, between neurotransmitters and hormones, the body was capable of operating and the brain of working.

All neurotransmitters were thought to be short, simple molecules, sometimes only a single amino acid long. They were released from one neuron, jumped across the synapse in milliseconds, and activated another neuron. Thus, they acted rapidly and had a single, specific target cell.

Hormones are much more complex than neurotransmitters. They are long chained peptides and are released by specialized groups of cells called glands. Adrenaline is produced by the adrenal glands and thyroxine by the thyroid gland. Hormones are released into the bloodstream and then must circulate through the blood system until they reach their target, generally, any number of different groups of cells. They take from minutes to hours to travel to their targets.

Both systems appear to be quite different in both origin and operation. Jeffery Barker characterizes neurotransmitters as being like lines that link one telephone with another. The message can only move along that line between those two phones. Dr. Barker then compares neurohormones to a radio broadcast. Anyone with a proper receiver can pick it up.

Within the past five years, the clear-cut division between neurotransmitter and *neurohormone* has broken down. Indeed, the same chemical can act as a neurotransmitter in one instance and as a neurohormone in the next. Nor is the molecular complexity or lack of it a trait of either group. Norepinephrine, first recognized as a neutrotransmitter and no more complicated than acetylcholine, turns out also to be a neurohormone. It is released by the adrenal glands. Vasopressin, a complicated peptide and a hormone, is now found to be a neurotransmitter located in the neurons of the hypothalamus. "Any human cell has the potential for producing a whole variety of hormonelike substances and also for developing a receptor system for them," Dr. Holmes observes. "And the brain probably uses all of them. All the gut hormones are going to turn out probably to be transmitters of the brain. Probably all of the known hormones and some of the suspected ones are going to turn out to be neurotransmitters in their spare time."

Does that mean there isn't any difference at all between these neurohormones acting as transmitters and the simple molecular neurotransmitters? Not at all. The short-chain transmitters affect neurons in one of two ways. They either turn them on or off by making it easier for sodium ions to get inside the nerve cell or by making it more difficult. The long-chain transmitters, however, do not directly affect the ability of the sodium ions to get into the neuron. Arriving at the nerve cell by themselves, these transmitters do nothing. They wait until a short-chain transmitter enters the scene. When the short-chain transmitter tries either to activate or deactivate the nerve cell, the long-chain transmitter sets up interference. The latter keeps the former from working as well as it should. The short-chain transmitter's function is not stopped, it is just slowed down. Thus, if the simple transmitter is supposed to turn on the nerve cell, the long-chain transmitter sees that this process takes longer than it normally would. If the short-chain transmitter is supposed to turn off the cell, again the more complicated transmitter sees that the process takes longer than normal.

If we think of acetylcholine and other simple neurotransmitters as a light switch and the neuron as a light bulb, we can see that these chemicals either turn the neuron on or off just as we would turn a light bulb on or off with the switch. The presence of the long-chain transmitter is like installing a dimmer switch. The neuron goes through a range of activity between on and off, just as our light bulb would go through a range of brightness as we twisted the dimmer.

All of this is interesting in what it tells us about the functioning of the brain on a cellular level. The new revolution in neurochemistry makes it obvious that the brain continues to be more complex than any previous model ever predicted. Certainly, the old "on/off" neuron theory has been increasingly pushed farther and farther into the background. Its importance to brain operation is still evident, but not as overriding as was once thought.

But what does this do for us now? What are the benefits? In the next two chapters, we shall see the roles that neurotransmitters and neurochemistry are going to be playing in the treatment of mental illness, chronic pain, Parkinson's disease, and other disorders traditionally handled by either psychiatric or surgical therapy. Beyond that is the promise of access through these chemicals to the slippery features of the mind. We may be on the verge of finding answers to the questions of what memory, learning, perhaps intelligence itself, are. We may also chemically be able to improve our individual performances with all these abilities.

The eventual goal of neurochemistry is the full understanding of the chemical operation of the brain, not just the control of pain or disease. The neurochemists could well be on the road to isolating the essence of consciousness itself. How soon will this be? Candace Pert feels that we will be seeing some positive benefits from the new neurochemistry before the turn of the century, less than twenty years in the future.

6

Troubleshooting the Neural Net: Mending the Brain

It is a special hospital, and it is busy. Patients come from all over the northern part of the state. Admissions and records send a constant demand for patient information to their computer. Down a corridor in Radiology, a CAT scanner is running. The images appearing on the monitor are being photographed, but the head of the department has already seen that the tumor is still small.

"Send the scans upstairs," he tells his technician, "and have them make a 3D of it, so we can see just how large it is."

"The PETT data just came in," the tech says, handing over a printout.

"Still, pretty inactive."

"Right. They'll probably be able to keep it under control with drugs for a while. So no surgery."

In another corridor, a young man stands shaking a small pill bottle. In it are two capsules. "I don't believe it," he tells another patient. "They said just two of these would take care of my back pain for the entire month."

In the hospital's south wing, a young women inserts a video cassette into a machine. On the monitor beside her, six lines appear. For a few minutes, the lines wiggle up and down. Nothing unusual. Then, there is a burst of intense activity. The lines run up and down the screen, seeming to go wild. She calls her chief.

"Two-seven in the morning," he says, looking at the time scale on the screen. "While he was asleep."

"No wonder he never knew he was having these attacks," says

the technician. "These twenty-four-hour monitoring EEG units are quite the miracle."

Downstairs, a group of men and women sit and watch the color display from a PETT. They are attentive, but not surprised. "The pattern definitely shows he's a manic-depressive, not a schizophrenic as they diagnosed in psych," says one of the women.

"That's why his treatment isn't working. Switch his medication, and he should be improving within the month," says the head doctor.

At the dispensary, a woman patient fingers the object the man behind the counter has just given her. "It looks like a piece of jewelry," she says.

"Sure. It is. But it's also a portable EEG. You wear that, and it will warn you in plenty of time before any *grand mal* seizure."

"But it's so pretty."

"Why not? Oh, yes sir," he says, turning to another patient who comes up to the counter, "here's your prescription. Follow the directions, and you should find your depression clearing up permanently."

Perhaps no such hospital as this, which specializes in brain disorders, will ever exist, but everything that it can do is now either possible or soon will be. The treatment of the brain has come a long way from the ancient Egyptians' crude tools for performing brain operations.

No one would claim that disease or injury to other parts of the body is not serious and is not deadly, but problems in the brain can and often do have more widespread effects. Also, treating the brain is difficult because of its complexity and its protective systems. These same systems often make it difficult even to find out what is wrong. Indeed, finding out what is wrong is sometimes as dangerous as the problem itself. But the modern doctor is not only aided by new machines such as the CAT and PETT scanners and surgical procedures, but also by a new understanding of the nature of both physical and mental disorders. An increased knowledge of the chemistry of the brain is leading to new insights into the nature and treatment of both pain and mental disorders such as schizophrenia.

The Tumor

Brain surgery is very old. The Incas and the Egyptians practiced it (read the novel *The Egyptian,* by Mika Waltari, for a vivid, if fictionalized, account of the Egyptian methods of brain surgery). De-

spite the difficulties in penetrating the skull, such surgery, if confined to the brain's surface, posed fewer hazards than did surgery of
the torso. There was less chance of infection (cut into the digestive
tract, and your patient's entire body could be be infected in a matter of
hours), and severing a major blood vessel was not a problem. Naturally, modern surgery has found ways of eliminating most of the risks of
conventional surgery. However, the reason for those ancient brain
surgeons still remains: the need to remove tumors.

A *tumor,* seeming to serve no known biological purpose, is a
clump of tissue that grows out of the cells surrounding it. It can either
be benign (harmless) or malignant (dangerous). Malignant tumors
need to be removed or they will kill the sufferer. A person with cancer
has one or more such tumors.

In the past, detection of tumors and the determination of their
placement in the brain as well as their size have been a combination
of long, uncomfortable searching, luck, and surgery. New techniques
in treatment, particularly the invention of the CAT scanner, now
increase a patient's survival time. In 1937, George Gershwin, the
composer of "Rhapsody in Blue," died five months after being diagnosed as having a brain tumor. According to Harry Schwartz in an
article in *The New York Times Magazine,* such tumors can be detected
earlier and treated more exactly with the use of the CAT scanner.
With the CAT scanner's sensitivity to different tissues, doctors can
now determine the presence of tumors as well as their exact size with
just a few rapid scans. Schwartz's own son led a mostly normal life for
three and a half years after his diagnosis for a brain tumor.

New techniques have made the examination of tumors and damage by stroke superior to those of even a few years ago. According to
one researcher, "We found if we inject some iodine, we can drastically
bring out the appearance of abnormal things such as tumors and
stroke areas. This is very, very dramatic since the structure under
observation lights up like a light bulb." Also, new computer technology allows doctors to have a CAT scan reprocessed so that it can be
seen in three dimensions. "Yes," says one neurosurgeon, "the Hunt-
ington Institute in Pasadena will not only send back the tumor scan
in 3-D, but also showing the number of millimeters the tumor measures."

Researchers at Johns Hopkins are working on methods of checking the nature of tumors with the CAT scanner. So far, scanning lung
tissue, they have seen that a certain growth with a low intensity
reading is malignant 80 percent of the time.

Still, the only reliable method for checking on whether or not a tumor is malignant is surgery. A slice of the suspect tissue is cut off and then tested. If the surgeon should slip with his scalpel, he could find himself cutting into and destroying perfectly healthy neurons. Neurosurgery today, however, is safer than at any time in the past and as sophisticated as any branch of surgery. New monitoring devices with readout screens for quick appraisal of a patient's condition and alarm signals if vital signs fall below an acceptable level, all add to the increased safety of cutting into the brain whether it be to grab a tumor specimen or to remove fully the tumor.

The success or failure of the operation, of course, depends upon the surgeon's skill. But modern surgeons perform much of the delicate cutting and suturing required in surgery on the brain using the operating microscope. Either a binocular, high-power microscope is swung out over the area of surgery or the surgeon wears special magnifying glasses. In either case, he is able to see specific details that his colleagues of twenty years ago would never have dreamed of.

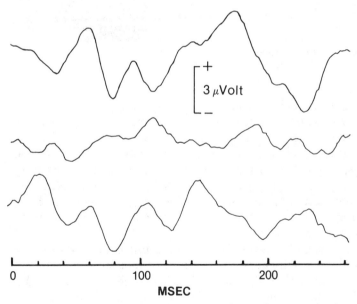

AEP recording monitoring patient's condition during operation. At top, the effect of anesthesia is shown. Middle pattern shows patient having trouble. Bottom recording shows a return to normal after problem is corrected. 3 μVolt = 0.000003 volt (three one-millionths of a volt), 100 msec = 0.1 second (one-tenth of a second). (Courtesy Nicolet Biomedical Instruments)

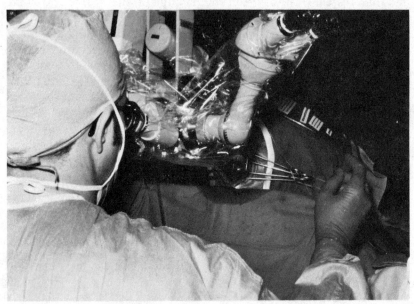

Microsurgery in which surgeon uses binocular microscope to perform delicate work. (Courtesy Nicolet Biomedical Instruments)

Once a tumor has been found to be malignant, it can be watched using the CAT scanner. If it is removed through surgery, periodic scans can show whether it is reforming and how rapidly it is growing. If chemical therapy is used, occasional scans can show whether the tumor is responding to treatment: whether it is shrinking, remaining the same size, or continuing to grow. When radiation is used, the radiation beam can be focused accurately using the information from the tomograms. This avoids exposing any more healthy tissue to radiation than is necessary.

However, the CAT scanner can only do so much. Since it can only look at function, it cannot show activity. It cannot pick up problems until after they have caused some structural damage. With the PETT scanners, doctors can monitor the actual growth and spread of a brain tumor. Since brain surgery is always risky, doctors prefer to postpone cutting tumors out as long as possible. Only when the tumor reaches a dangerous size is surgery scheduled. With the PETT, the chemical activity of the tumor can be watched. When it increases to a certain level, the risk posed by the tumor outweighs the dangers of surgery.

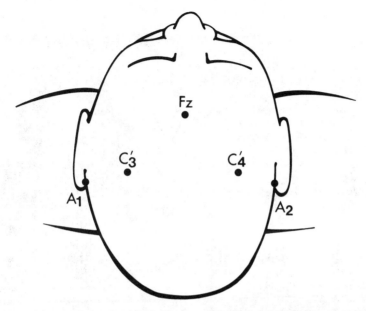

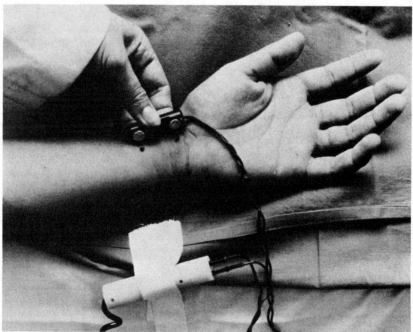

Placement of electrodes on scalp and on wrist for surgical AEP monitoring. (Courtesy Nicolet Biomedical Instruments)

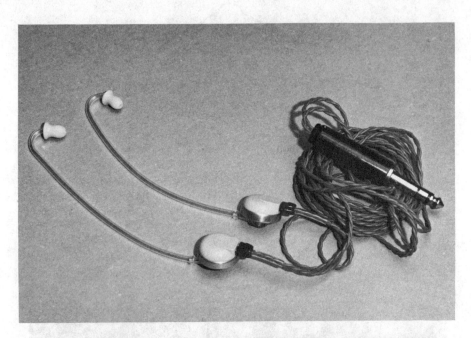

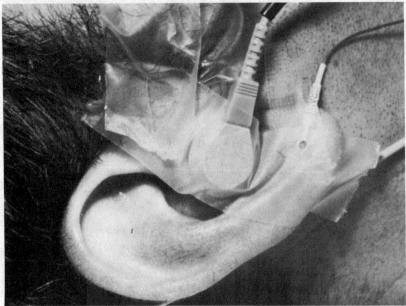

Auditory stimulator electrodes for AEP surgical monitoring.   (Courtesy Nicolet Biomedical Instruments)

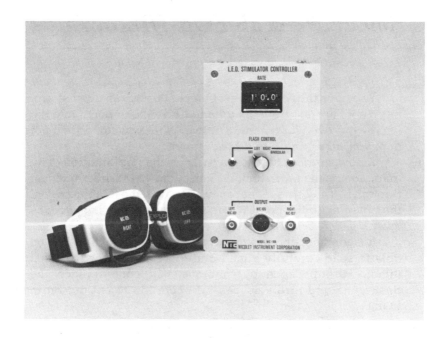

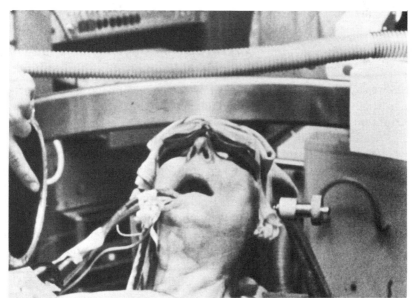

(Top) Visual AEP surgical stimulator with control unit. (Bottom) Patient with stimulators in place during operation. (Courtesy Nicolet Biomedical Instruments)

MICROWAVES FOR THE BRAIN

You have thirty minutes for lunch. So you run downstairs, buy a cold hot dog from the automatic deli, and pop it into the microwave oven for a minute or two. What you can do to a hot dog, you also can do to a brain tumor.

A new surgical technique calls for the implantation of an antenna into the brain tumor. Then microwaves are broadcast through it. They spread just enough to send the temperature of the tumor up to the point where its internal chemistry breaks down.

Researchers are already working on a helmet that will be able to send carefully aimed and directed microwaves at a tumor. Perhaps such a technique will soon replace the dangerous and rarely successful operation to cut out brain tumors.

Epilepsy

As we saw in Chapter 1, epilepsy has been a recognized brain disorder for thousands of years. The violence of the *grand mal* is often frightening, and even the milder *petit mal* can be disturbing.

Detecting epilepsy is not always a simple matter. True, an EEG of a seizure is quite characteristic (see Chapter 2, Figure 4), but recording sessions do not always produce evidence of epilepsy. The sessions only occur every day or so and last from one to two hours. If the patient does not have a seizure during those sessions, the nature of the epilepsy and its severity may be difficult to determine. But chance no longer need play a role in EEG monitoring. Now, the patient is given a small EEG amplifier with electrodes and leads. The unit is small enough to fit into a convenient pouch so that the person can carry the unit with him at work, during the evening, and at night he can place it on his bedstand.

An EEG record is made on videocassettes, which are taken back to the doctor, who then plays them. He can follow the patient's brain

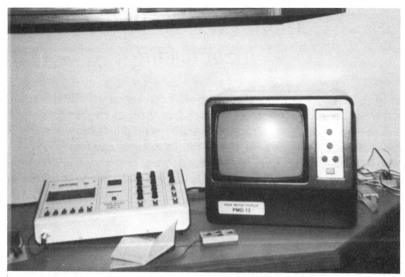

Oxford PMD-12 monitor for portable EEG unit. The cassette is inserted into playback unit, and the technician can watch the brain waves on the TV screen. (Courtesy Neurological Associates)

waves for every twenty-four period, and whatever unusual activity might happen during that period will be his to examine.

The idea is so good that a manufacturer of biomedical jewelry is planning to market a small EEG detector. The jewelry so far has been confined to necklaces that warn of excessive ultraviolet light or heavy air pollution. But, a small, attractive EEG recorder would be of immense popularity since it would do the job of the larger bulky units of today, but it would not label the person carrying it as being ill.

The PETT also is particularly good for detecting epilepsy. Scans show the areas damaged by such seizures, but they also show not only the point at which the seizure began, but in which direction it spread. Oddly enough, between seizures, the point of origin shows less activity than the normal nerve cells. Since some forms of epilepsy can only be cured through surgery, the PETT can locate the exact neurons to be cut out. The surgeon can go directly to those strangely inactive cells.

One of the purposes of neurosurgery is the insertion of devices to correct the malfunctioning brain. Recently, a small, battery-operated *brain pacemaker* has been placed in the brain of epileptics. The pacemaker sits in the center of the origin of the seizure. When it detects the first surge of the wild firing that initiates the epileptic attack, the pacemaker sets up a counter current and stops the seizure dead.

Mental Illness and Schizophrenia

Mental illness, the mad, the insane. These concepts, illnesses, and sufferers have been the object of much fear through the centuries. Nor is that fear a thing of the past. We still are afraid of the mentally ill and hide them away as best we can in institutions and rest homes. If a friend or relative has to be hospitalized for *schizophrenia* or one of the other mental diseases, we talk little of it. We try not to think about them, try to push them out of our minds—just the opposite of what we do for someone who is in the hospital for a heart operation or recovering from a broken leg. And despite the increase in the number of psychologists and psychiatrists, we still feel that there is something wrong with consulting such people. Just look at the number of uneasy jokes about these professions.

But the mentally ill represent a very serious health problem. Schizophrenia, often called the cancer of mental disorders, claims large numbers of victims a year. It is one of the most widespread diseases in the world. Fortunately, our squeamishness is not preventing much needed work being done for finding cures for the sufferers of these brain disorders.

And what is schizophrenia, this cancer of mental disorders? The word itself means split mind, but it does not mean the sufferer has a split or multiple personality. Rather, schizophrenics act as though one part of their mind has seized control of the whole brain. The unity of the mind has broken down, and the schizophrenic loses contact with reality. He or she often suffers from hallucinations and feelings of persecution, sometimes completely withdrawing within him or herself.

Schizophrenia, like all mental disorders, can be difficult to diagnose. The diagnosis depends upon the observation of the patient's behavior by a trained psychiatrist. Such an evaluation, no matter how practiced the doctor, can hardly be called objective. Even the progress of treatment is subjective. The patient meets periodically with his doctor, and the doctor decides how well the schizophrenic's condition is responding to treatment. Needless to say, mistakes are sometimes made.

The PETT scanner may offer a solution. J. Eric Holmes, who feels that the future of body scanners will be a machine that can produce a three-dimensional holographic projection of a brain slice, says, "I'd love to see such a scanner for a schizophrenic brain. Particularly one in the process of getting better as well as one that's being treated."

Such a holographic scanner is still in the future, but the look at the schizophrenic brain is not. Alfred Wolf of Brookhaven National Laboratory has been making tomograms of schizophrenics as well as *manic-depressives*. Manic-depressives, suffering from a different type of mental disorder than the schizophrenic, swing through a cycle of almost uncontrollable exuberance, followed by deep, sometimes suicidal depressions. The treatments for both disorders are different. Since diagnosis is no easier for manic-depression than schizophrenia, costly mistakes can be made.

Dr. Wolf has discovered that both schizophrenics and manic-depressives give very distinctive tomograms. They not only differ from those of the normal brain, but also from each other. The schizophrenic's brain scan shows a marked decrease in the take-up of 2-deoxyglucose, the radioactive tracer, in the frontal lobes. Manic-depressives in their manic phase use an abnormally large amount of the tracer all over the brain. In the depressive phase, the scan unfortunately shows nothing different from the normal brain.

Wolf has further shown that treatment of both conditions can be watched using the PETT scanner. One schizophrenic was put on a drug, perpenazine, which is often used for treating this disorder. Over a period of several weeks, tomograms of his brain showed an increase in the 2-deoxyglucose in the frontal lobes. As the brain scan came to look more normal, so did the patient's behavior.

Another of Wolf's subjects was diagnosed as being schizophrenic. When Wolf ran a scan of the subject, however, he discovered that the brain pattern was that of a manic-depressive. The patient was put on lithium, a common control for manic-depression, and is reportedly getting along much better.

If Wolf's work proves effective, at least detection and monitoring of the mentally ill, the manic-depressives, and the schizophrenics will be made more reliable. Unfortunately, treatment for most mental disorders, particularly schizophrenia, has been relatively hit-or-miss. As one neurobiologist comments, "It is totally blind what you can do for people stuck in mental hospitals or in and out of such hospitals. They give them a variety of drugs, which seem to have an effect over and above any side effect, so the drugs are continued to be used." Indeed, although drugs have been used in controlling mental illness for thirty years, prescription of such drugs is mainly try-it-with-each-patient. If it works, continue with it, if not, go to another drug.

The problem is beginning to yield to some basic knowledge which is getting at the cause of schizophrenia and manic-depression. What does cause schizophrenia? The most common belief until the 1970's was environment. An unpleasant childhood, an unsettling experience at a susceptible age, and the person might seek withdrawal from the nastiness of reality. The problem with this explanation comes when you realize that many people have had bad childhoods. But most do not go schizophrenic or become depressive.

Psychologists are now leaning more and more to the idea that mental illness has physical causes just as much as, say, an appendicitis. Something goes wrong with the chemial and structural workings of the brain's neurons. The search for a chemical cause of schizophrenia began in the mid-1950's. However, even before that, evidence existed that this disorder possibly had a chemical origin. In 1943 in Basel, Switzerland, a chemist, Albert Hoffman, accidentally swallowed a small quantity of *d-lysergic acid diethylamide, LSD*. He had to be taken home after he began violently hallucinating. His symptoms were quite similar to those of the schizophrenic. A decade later, LSD was discovered to tie up the enzyme that reacted with another chemical found in the human body and brain, *serotonin*. The theory at the time was that serotonin, no longer able to react normally, formed abnormal chemical compounds which caused schizophrenia. This is a reasonable theory since an abnormal adrenaline compound had been shown to cause temporary deranged behavior in normal human volunteers. This adrenaline compound does not naturally occur within the human body. Neither, unfortunately, as far as anyone could tell, do the suspected compounds from serotonin, even in schizophrenics.

More recently, however, studies with LSD have indicated that the schizophrenic state it induces is through a very complex series of reactions that involve not only serotonin, but adrenaline, noradrenaline, and several other body chemicals. As we saw in the last chapter, studying the biochemistry of the human brain is very difficult and very time consuming. With time, we will know the exact mechanism of LSD and, we hope, schizophrenia.

However, the neurochemists are not merely studying one set of chemicals for the source of schizophrenia. They are also looking for a possible neurotransmitter that could cause this disorder. And the evidence is there. The limbic system, the old part of our brain, is the seat of our emotional control. Here a neurotransmitter called *dopamine* has receptor sites. In schizophrenics, dopamine has been found in excessive amounts in the limbic system. The postulate is that this neurotransmitter runs amok in this region of the brain, upsetting the emotional balance of the schizophrenic. And schizophrenia is a disease of emotional imbalance. Further, dopamine is also produced in the lower reaches of the cerebrum, which controls body movement; however, in schizophrenics, the dopamine levels in this part of the brain are normal. The only abnormality is in the limbic system.

Examination of the limbic system has also shown that the neurons are often malformed or reveal signs of destruction. The dopamine apparently attacks the cells of the brain. Thus, schizophrenia does arise from actual, physical damage. The obvious first step was to try blocking dopamine production. With mild cases of schizophrenia, some improvement was seen. But severe cases showed no signs of recovery. Perhaps the cellular damage is too great for these severe cases. Or, as has been put forth, excessive dopamine production is only one part of the overall chemical imbalance in the schizophrenic. What these new chemicals might be is still a mystery. Possibly they are serotonin, adrenaline, and noradrenaline.

The time may come when every newborn baby is checked for an excess of dopamine and the other chemicals linked to schizophrenia. Such procedures already exist for the detection of phenylketonuria, a chemical imbalance that leads to mental retardation, in which simple, regular injections of a needed enzyme eliminate any brain damage. So, in the future, babies who show the imbalances that lead to schizophrenia will receive injections. The mental illness equivalent of cancer will then be as much a thing of the past as smallpox is today.

Parkinson's Disease

Dopamine has also been linked with another mental disorder, Parkinson's disease (see Chapter 1, Sidebar 2). As Dr. J. Eric Holmes says, "There is a strange relationship between schizophrenia and Parkinson's. If you have schizophrenia, we give you a drug that might give you Parkinsonism. If you have Parkinsonism, we give you a bunch of drugs that normally do not give you schizophrenia, but . . . . There's a relationship. They're all tied together by their biochemistry."

Above we saw that dopamine is also produced in the part of the cerebrum controlling body movement. However, where an excess of dopamine in the limbic system seems to produce schizophrenia, a deficiency of it seems to produce Parkinson's in this part of the cerebrum. Why not just inject dopamine into the bloodstream and wait for it to find those receptors starving for it in the brain? A good idea, but dopamine can't get into the brain from the bloodstream.

However, a combination of dopamine and another drug produces a chemical, *L-dopa,* which could get into the brain and seek out those receptor sites. Unfortunately, L-dopa has side effects. In advanced sufferers of Parkinson's, it causes an on again, off again reaction. The person will seem perfectly normal for a time. Then, he will become rigid for a while.

Eric Holmes suggests that an Ommaya Reservoir might be able to deliver dopamine to the needed receptors. An Ommaya Reservoir is a "drug-injecting mechanism that's used in cases where, over a long period of time, you have to administer some antibiotic to the brain. You could arrange it so you are injecting dopamine directly into the brain." A tube would run from the skull to the area of the cerebrum that is dopamine poor. In the skull, you would place a rubber stopper that's inserted into a small vial. The tube would be connected to this vial. The skin of the scalp over the stopper would be sewed back up. Then dopamine would be injected through the stopper into the vial. From the vial, the chemical would trickle down and out to the brain.

Probably one of the most ambitious projects for the future is the *neural graft.* Experiments with mice that have been treated so they have an artificial form of Parkinson's disease have shown that grafting healthy neural tissue into the dopamine-poor regions has some effect. The tissue for grafting is gotten from mice fetuses from the same part of the brain as is damaged in the adult mice.

Doctors think a similar neural grafting would work in humans. The problem is getting the tissue to make the graft. The best source is fetal brain tissue since adult tissue just shrivels up and dies. However, the ethical problems involved in taking tissue from human fetuses is a major stumbling block to this treatment, a treatment that might work for other disorders arising from specific neural damages.

Is there an alternative? Aborted fetuses are not usable, but oddly enough for Parkinson's, tissue from the adrenal glands can be used. It is very similar to nervous tissue and when put into a mouse's brain takes on the characteristics of the surrounding tissue. However, this may not work for other damaged neurons. The ultimate answer is to be able to clone human neural tissue. With such a procedure, only those particular cells which were needed could be grown. They could then be grafted into the brain to take over the malfunctioning neurons.

Chronic Pain

Pain is felt everywhere in the body except the brain. Cut your finger, and it hurts. Cut into the brain tissue, however, and you experience no sensation of pain. Indeed, brain surgery is often performed with the patient awake and conscious. Brain surgery is one of the oldest forms of internal surgery, undoubtedly because the patient would not be thrashing around in pain.

Then what about headaches? Headaches are caused by pressure on the membranes, the dura mater, the arachnoid membrane, and the pia mater, surrounding the brain. During brain surgery, a local anesthetic is used to dull the pain receptors of the scalp and these membranes.

Ironically, although the brain does not itself feel pain, it is the organ that senses pain. Your cut finger does not actually hurt at the site of the cut. It may indeed feel as though it is throbbing, but in fact, the entire sensation of pain is contained within the thalamus, located at the base of the cerebrum.

Traditionally, pain has been minimized or eliminated through the use of local anesthetics or the administration of drugs. Anyone who has had a tooth filled or pulled has been injected with novocaine, which deadens the pain receptors in the gums and in the nerve of the tooth. Most of us have used some kind of non-prescription drug such as aspirin for headaches. Such relief is quite adequate for temporary pain. Indeed, few industries are as large and prosperous as that devoted to pain relief. Unfortunately, for anything except temporary pain, the various drugs and anesthetics are either partially or wholly ineffective.

As we saw in the fourth chapter, pain, unlike other sensory input, does not fade from the conscious mind. If the problem causing the pain cannot be corrected, then the receptors will continue to send impulses to the brain, which in turn will continue to receive and act upon them. On the whole, this system is sensible. Pain is a warning that something is wrong with our bodies, so if the brain could ignore these warnings, we could easily find ourselves forgetting to take care of serious threats to ourselves. However, some problems such as bad backs or arthritis cannot be corrected, and the pain can range from unpleasant to unbearable and incapacitating, serving no apparent useful purpose. So, what can be done about long-lasting, recurring, or permanent pain?

In the past pain sufferers had to find what relief they could in stronger, prescription drugs, surgery, physical therapy, and so on.

Pain can often also be totally eliminated by the severing of nerves leading from the injured body region to the brain. This, however, leaves the patient unable to control or feel anything in, say, an arm or leg. In the earlier part of the century, doctors relieved chronic pain through prefrontal lobotomies, the surgical division of the front part of the cerebrum from the back part. These patients reported that, although they were still aware of the pain, they no longer cared about its presence. This passivity was characteristic of such operations, which generally left the patient mentally deficient, a grave price to pay for pain relief.

Drugs, of course, have been the most effective means of stopping pain. Unfortunately, the most effective also have serious side effects or are addictive. No drug is as able to eliminate pain from the conscious mind as heroin, but the cost to the individual is often as serious as it is from some surgical cures. But what about inside the brain itself, where the pain impulses are actually received? Can the brain give us an answer to effective, but harmless pain relief? Yes, is the answer of those now studying neurochemistry, the chemistry of the brain. When we will be able to accomplish such interior pain control is not quite so clear.

After the discovery of endorphin and enkephalin, physicians hoped that injections of these chemicals or their synthetics would be the universal pain relievers of the future. Will endorphin and enkephalin be the miracle drugs of tomorrow? No, at least not by simple injection. When injected into lab animals, both compounds proved to be as addictive as heroin. Neurochemists even tried creating similar chemicals. Although these substitutes worked as well as the original, they also were as addictive. So, direct use of endorphin and enkephalin for pain relief was out.

But the two opiates are already present in the brain, and the machinery that manufactures them in the pituitary is available. Perhaps, then, the biochemists reasoned, the answer is not to introduce additional endorphin or enkephalin from outside the body. Rather it should be possible to cause the brain to make more of the two chemicals itself.

In 1978, Seymour Ehrenpreis of the Chicago Medical School developed a drug, *d-phenylalanine, DPA* for short, that interferes with the enzyme responsible for breaking down enkephalin. So, remove this enzyme and the enkephalin already present remains. To that is then added more enkephalin. The end result is an increase in the amount of enkephalin in the brain. More enkephalin means more pain-fighting ability on the brain's part. And, perhaps, best of all, none of the 200 mice tested showed any addictive behavior.

How much of the DPA would be needed to take care of the permanent pain from rheumatism or advanced cancer? Very little, indeed a surprisingly small amount. As few as two pills a month would be sufficient to keep enkephalin levels high enough to fight successfully chronic pain. So, in the not-too-distant future, perhaps we should expect to be sent by our doctor to the druggist when we are in pain. There, we will be given a pill vial with two small capsules. The instructions will read, "Take one every twenty-four hours. Refill in one month."

Nor are endorphin and enkephalin the only painkillers found in the brain. Solomon Snyder and others at Johns Hopkins have isolated another small, thirteen-amino-acid chain called *neurotensin*. Neurotensin is found in the part of the brain that pulls together information about pain and emotion. Its exact role is not yet known, but it is about 1,000 times more effective than enkephalin at reducing

---

TENS

Neurochemistry does not offer the only method for pain control. A recent invention, the Transcutaneous Electrical Nerve Stimulator—the TENS unit—offers many relief from pain.

The TENS is a small battery-operated rectangular box that can be slipped into a pocket. The sufferer can carry it with him anywhere and everywhere. Leading from the box are two wires ending in electrodes mounted into sticky pads. The pads are placed on the skin just over the area of pain. When the unit is activated, the pain soon disappears. The TENS sends a barrage of electrical signals along the nervous system. These TENS-inspired currents compete and generally defeat the pain impulses.

Although the unit does not work for everyone, it has been successfully used, instead of medication, to eliminate pain after operations. And some people with chronic pain such as sciatica and even arthritis find relief with the TENS unit. Until the neurochemists can produce a chemical cure for long-term pain, the TENS will do nicely according to its users.

pain. It also appears to be nonaddictive. So, neurochemistry has provided a second possible agent in the fight against chronic pain.

But there is a third possibility: attack the actual chemical that transmits pain. As early as 1931, two researchers, Ulf S. von Euler and John H. Goddum, discovered such a chemical. They called it *substance P*. P because it was a certain preparation and was in a powder form. But now P stands for pain. Substance P, like acetylcholine, is a neurotransmitter. When a pain receptor in the skin is activated, the nerve impulse travels down the nerve fiber. Substance P is the chemical that leaps the synapse (see Figure 1). Substance P then plays an important role in getting that pain signal to the thalamus. However, substance P has turned out to be limited to carrying a specific type of pain. It is not the universal pain neurotransmitter. There is no such thing. So, now neurochemists are looking for the others.

Montford Piercey showed that substance P's role is the transmittal of chemical pain. Piercey injected mice with a substance that keeps substance P from working. He then sprinkled the skin of the mice with a red-hot pepper derivative. The mice did not react with pain. When he applied heat, however, they did show pain. Thus, a different transmitter is responsible for carrying messages of burns to the brain. The chemical block that Piercey used is an altered form of substance P itself. So, here we have a third possible chemical agent against recurring pain. If the brain's own defenses against pain cannot be turned loose by neurochemists, perhaps it can be isolated from feelings of pain. Stop the pain neurotransmitters, and the brain has no way of sensing pain.

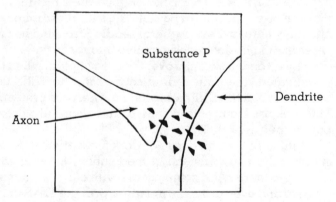

Figure 1. Substance P crossing synapse to activate a neuron.

Piercey's preparation is not yet practical. First, it must be injected directly into the spine. When injected into the bloodstream, it cannot get into the brain (the brain's protective systems keep it away from the neurons). Spinal injections are more complicated and more painful than those into a vein. And certainly, you could not do one by yourself at home as a diabetic can inject himself with insulin. The second problem is the chemical's survival time. Within five minutes of its being injected, enzymes attack it and destroy it. Obviously, the lifetime of this substance P block must be increased to several hours before it will be a useful pain remedy.

But, these are technical problems. In the future, we may see this chemical marketed in infinitely small time-release capsules such as are used for cold drugs like Contac. They will be made up of substances that can easily slip through the brain's chemical fence around the neurons. Then, over a period of hours, perhaps days, each small capsule will release its tiny portion of the substance P block, and the pain will end.

Obviously, the miracle pain killer is still a thing of the future. Yet, that future is not far from us. If Seymour Ehrenpreis's DPA does not provide a cure for pain, perhaps neurotensin or Piercey's substance P inhibitor will. Of maybe, and this is most likely, a combination of all three will turn the trick. But an answer is visible on the horizon of neurochemical research.

Chemistry is being helped by neurosurgery. In the section on epilepsy, we saw how surgeons were placing brain pacemakers in the center of the seizure areas. This is not the only type of implant being tested. A neurosurgeon, Yoshio Hosobuchi, of the University of California at San Francisco, has developed an endorphin stimulator. Several small electrodes are placed into the region near the thalamus. Wires lead from the electrodes to the chest, where they end in a receiver. The receiver is located just beneath the surface of the skin.

A small radio transmitter will turn on the receiver. The receiver, in turn, activates the electrodes, which then stimulate endorphin production. So, when a chronic pain sufferer has an attack, he turns on his transmitter and waits about fifteen minutes. Relief is quickly on its way.

Unfortunately, not everyone responds to this device, but for those who do, it is effective. Perhaps the day will come when such implants and such techniques are not needed. But for the moment, our technology is providing us with methods of overcoming and treating brain disorders that ten years ago were thought to be permanent.

The Unruly Brain

When we speak of mending the brain, we are speaking of more than just the damage done by disease or injury. Difficulty with memory, learning, and thinking may in the future yield to neurochemical solutions. Indeed, problems with behavior, which reflect a problem within our brains, may soon disappear through the use of the proper dosage of the correct neurotransmitter or neurohormone. According to one researcher, "Clinical tests are being performed on an anti-obesity agent, which apparently has no side effects." If such a drug could control our urge to overeat, it would earn its place in many of our hearts, if for no other reason, by putting an end to the countless diet books that now fill bookstore shelves.

Further, mending our brains may help cure problems in the rest of our bodies. All our bodily functions are controlled from the brain, so if something goes wrong in the brain, it will have an adverse effect somewhere in the body.

One of the major problems in this country is high blood pressure. And, although not as common, there are those who suffer from low blood pressure. Research reported by Richard Wurtman indicates that specific chemicals such as *tyrosine* can affect the operation of brain systems. Indeed, tyrosine has been shown to control both high and low blood pressure (see Figure 2). When tyrosine is given to lab animals with high blood pressure, it stimulates the production of the neurotransmitter norepinephrine. This transmitter slows down the

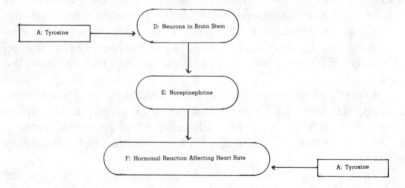

Figure 2.   The amino acid tyrosine can lower high blood pressure and can raise low blood pressure.

neurons controlling blood pressure, so the pressure falls. In animals with low blood pressure, the tyrosine blocks the effect of the norepinephrine. Since this latter cannot now slow up the neurons controlling blood pressure, they continue to work, raising the blood pressure. If blood pressure is normal, tyrosine has no effect.

And where can we get tyrosine? In our diet. Many foods are high in it, and it can be bought. Think what it would be like to walk from your doctor's office to the grocery store. There you would buy the specific nutritional chemicals he had recommended to take care of your blood pressure problems. No drugs at all.

Indeed, according to Wurtman, such chemicals can even eliminate problems due to actual neuron damage. These chemicals do not themselves directly affect anything. Instead, they are used by the cells in the brain to manufacture other chemicals that do the actual work.

And their effect? Healthy nerve cells normally fire a set number

YOUNGER BRAINS IN OLD BODIES?

Want to learn a new language? If you are four, you will have no trouble. If you are twelve, you will probably find it hard work.

So, how can we make our brains younger, bring back that plasticity? According to Takuji Kasamatsu of the California Institute of Technology, by using a common neurotransmitter: norepinephrine.

Kasamatsu tested his theory by taking adult cats, sewing one eye shut, and injecting them with the transmitter. He found that the chemical brought the cats back to the mental flexibility of kittens. He was able to teach these adult cats with norepinephrine as easily and as quickly to adjust to monocular vision as he was able to do with kittens.

So, in the future, you may go to your local health food store and stock up on norepinephrine just before those big exams or before starting that correspondence course.

of times per second, let's say five (a very slow set of neurons). Thus, in one area of the brain, if you have a set of two neurons that feed into four others, the two will release ten neurotransmitters with each second of firing. These transmitters will set off the other four, and the process continues (see Figure 3). If something happens to one of the leading neurons and three of the others, you have a fall in the neural activity. For a while, the two remaining neurons try to keep up with the old firing pattern and the number of neurotransmitters released. But they can't do it; they fall behind.

However, if the right chemical is eaten by the person with this damaged neuron system, that chemical will be used by the remaining neurons to make more transmitters. Thus, the two neurons can, with additional material, keep up the same level of activity as before the damage. What happens if you eat this basic chemical and no neurons have been hurt? Nothing. The system only responds when there is need.

	Number of Neurons	Number of Firings	Quantity of Neurotransmitter
A	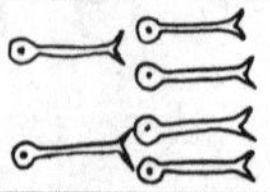	Normal	Sufficient
B		Above Normal	Insufficient
C		Above Normal	Sufficient

Figure 3. The addition of the right chemical can help a damaged neuron system. Here, A shows the undamaged neurons firing normally and producing sufficient quantities of neurotransmitter. B shows the damaged neurons firing many times more than normal, but failing to produce sufficient quantities of neurotransmitter. C shows the damaged neurons after the chemical additive, still firing above normal but now producing sufficient quantities of neurotransmitter.

THE NEGATIVE IS THE POSITIVE

Ever felt depressed, moody, irritable? Of course you have. Everyone does occasionally, but the cause may be as simple as the wind outside.

Dry, hot winds such as the Chinook in the Rockies are accompanied by increases in violence and depression. Why? These winds blow in large quantities of positive ions and drive out the negative ions.

Experiments with rats have shown that those raised in air heavy with negative ions have not only larger brains, but sleep better. They are also less irritable. Indeed, people who use negative ion generators report that they feel better and are not as consumed with stress.

Negative ions appear to lower the levels of a neurotransmitter, serotonin, which is suspected of being one of the chemical agents in depression.

So, it would appear that the negative is the positive.

7

Seeking the Light Fantastic: Mind and Brain

"I think, therefore, I am," said René Descartes. Despite his having written this in the seventeenth century, Descartes captured the essence of our present concept of the mind: thinking and being. We usually use the word *mind* to refer to certain qualities that reside in the brain that have no physical reality for us: intelligence, memory, learning, and, perhaps most elusive of all, consciousness, that awareness in each of us that we exist as separate, living organisms. The study of the mind is undoubtedly the most frustrating and difficult of any area in brain research. Indeed, less is known about the mind and its workings than is known about any other function of the human brain. The mind will be the last thing the brain scientist masters.

At present even the nature of the mind remains unknown. One group sees the mind as an independent, nonphysical "substance." For them the mind exists, and then comes the brain. For a second group, the brain is the source and creator of the mind. The brain's chemical and electrical processes and its physical structure give body and character to the mind. Without the brain, there is no mind. As Michael Phelps of UCLA observes, "The mind represents the function of the brain." A third group, and the most recent, views the mind as an information processing system. To them, anything, whether it be the human brain or the most advanced computer, has a mind if it can take in data, rework it, and send it out again in an altered form.

Probably no one of these groups is completely right or completely wrong. The answer may lie somewhere among them, or it may lie with an entirely new system. But, the mind is the greatest challenge the brain offers the neuroresearcher. It is a challenge that is being met in today's labs.

The PETT scanner is one tool that may enable scientists to study both the brain and the mind, and their interrelationship. Says Michael Phelps of UCLA: "Positron tomography is in fact a new technique that steps in between the neurochemical approach and the behavioral approach. . . . Since positron tomography measures the function of the brain, it is also looking at the way in which the mind functions. Now there are obvious limitations in that. We are looking at chemical changes that occur when you do things. The psychologist or psychiatrist might say there are tremendous limitations to that." Yet Phelps sees positron tomography as "a method for objectively measuring how the brain handles all its input from sight to the cognitive processing."

Phelps would not claim that he or his colleagues with or without the PETT and other instruments have even begun to define and characterize the human mind. But the results from such research are tantalizing and mark some of the first real progress in grappling with the question of what our minds are and how they work.

Some of the best examples of the physical relationship between brain and mind are those studying memory and learning. Although neither concept is synonymous with the other, learning without memory is impossible. We are not talking about the old rote memory that we used to remember multiplication tables but rather the important memory that allows us to remember the sequence of doing long division or subtraction. Here learning and memory are so tightly intertwined that we cannot separate them.

What do we know about learning and consequently its connection with the mind and the brain? Traditionally, schools have presented students with fairly structured programs to learn reading, mathematics, history, science, and so on. Educators have experimented with various approaches from student-to-student teaching, to teaching machines, to even new subjects. Some of these methods have helped, some have not. But to find out what is going on in the brain, we have to go to the neurobiologists rather than the educators. Perhaps in the future the two approaches, education and neuroresearch, will come together. David Hubel seems to feel that "If you understand how learning works, you can understand a lot more about education."

The Chemical Rewards of Learning and Remembering

What has been learned about the neurotransmitter system and its relation to memory and learning?

You feel a rush of excitement. You have just discovered something you never knew, and you find it fascinating. Your excitement continues building as you dig around the library and learn more and more about this new subject. Eventually, your initial exhilaration gives way to a calmer, quieter contentment as your initial burst of exploration gives way to a time of reflection. You ponder and analyze what you have learned, and it becomes part of your memory.

Such feelings are common to most of us, and they are linked with two different neurotransmitter systems. Our learning and memory are tied to the sense of satisfaction that the enkephalin-endorphin system and the norepinephrine system can bring us. Studies with rats done by Larry Stein and James D. Belluzzi of Wyeth Laboratories revealed this two step chemical nature of learning and memory. Rats were taught that the wire mesh covering the bottom of their cages would electrically shock them. Some of the rats were injected with endorphin; the remainder weren't. Then the electric shocks were stopped. Those rats without endorphin forgot more quickly about the shock they had been receiving than those who had endorphin. The endorphin appeared to heighten memory.

Stein and Belluzzi theorize that memory and learning have at their base a reward system. The brain rewards the individual for learning and remembering things by increasing the endorphin or enkephalin level. Thus, if you learn and remember well, you get an internal shot that makes you feel good.

The same good feeling comes also from norepinephrine. In rats, the equivalent of this neurotransmitter, like endorphin, increased memory length. Norepinephrine gives rise to the initial excitement in learning and remembering. This chemical rewards you for singling out the information that is most important to you from all the information before you. For selecting well, you are rewarded by your brain.

Endorphin and enkephalin are responsible for the milder, quieter excitement that follows the norepinephrine rush. No matter how much you want to learn about some subject, eventually you have to stop and think about what you have been learning. It is as important as the other experience, or too much information will flood your brain and wash away the significance of what you have been studying. So, again, you are rewarded. This time by this second neurochemical system when you rest for a while.

The Physical Site of Memory and Learning

In 1978, two scientists, O'Keefe and Nadel, reported on some work done with the *hippocampus* in rats. The hippocampus? According to J. Eric Holmes, in humans, "The hippocampus is in the temporal lobe [see Figure 1]. It's a fairly big area that has a funny anatomy with an incredibly horrible nomenclature. It also has extensive connections with the hypothalamus." This might be the site of learning, perhaps even intelligence.

O'Keefe and Nadel did to the hippocampus what Hubel and Wiesel did to the vision pathway (see Chapter 4). They inserted microelectrodes into individual cells. Then they monitored the firing of these cells as the rats ran mazes or just explored the laboratory. A rat would come to a right turn in a maze, and a single neuron would fire. It would come to a left turn, and another nerve cell activated.

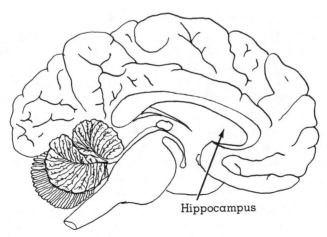

Hippocampus

Figure 1. Location of the hippocampus, possible site of learning and decision making.

Another right turn, and a third cell unrelated to the first two fired. O'Keefe and Nadel concluded they were recording the making of decisions. And this recording was on a single-cell basis within the confines of a specific region of the brain. They felt that the hippocampus contained a map of the maze and the lab. This map's coordinates were contained within each individual cell.

As Dr. Holmes observes, "From this, they made the intuitive leap to saying that in humans the hippocampus is a conceptual, verbalized mass of language, knowledge, everything else that a person knows. Located cell by cell. Whether this hangs together or not, it is an exciting possibility." Is there any basis for this "intuitive leap" on O'Keefe and Nadel's part? What is known about the *human* hippocampus? Well, for one thing, injury to the hippocampus in people seems to cause some memory loss. Certainly, without memory, learning is impossible. You have to be able not only to hold information you learn, but to recall it later. If you can't do this, you can't use the information. You have not learned.

But what type of memory loss are we talking about? Total amnesia? No. The man or woman with the injured hippocampus can still speak, can still remember events prior to his or her accident, and indeed, seems quite normal, particularly to strangers. But this person can no longer remember new information. Take, as Dr. Holmes suggests, such a person. He is in a car accident and is taken to a nearby hospital. Recovering consciousness, the man asks, "Where am I?"

"Northwest General" is the answer. He nods.

A minute later, he again asks where he is and is given the same answer. No matter how many times he is told "Northwest General," he will be unable to remember it. No amount of repetition will make him remember that name. Indeed, later, if he should wander away from his bed and his ward, he will be unable to remember where they are. "He doesn't know the name of the patient in the next bed. He doesn't know anything you've tried to teach him in all that period. His memory problem is immense," concludes Dr. Holmes. "But he has relatively few other neurological problems." If the hippocampus does indeed turn out to be where we learn, perhaps in the future, we will be able to feed data directly into this part of the brain through implanted electrodes. Do you want to learn Italian, then plug up the teaching cassette and let the lessons flow into the hippocampus. Let the cells responsible for learning language receive the Italian without it having to go through the long process of passing down the canal of the ear, along the auditory nerve, through the brain stem, up to the auditory area of the cerebrum, and then down to the hippocampus.

Perhaps, synthetic neurotransmitters can also be made that will heighten sensitivity of, say, the cells that control learning mathematics. So, before going to algebra class, you pop a math capsule. Your hippocampus then is ready to take the lesson for the day and record it where you can have it for your next exam.

The Whole Solution

So far, we have been talking about memory and learning as functions of specific regions of the brain. However, the mind-brain relationship is probably nowhere near this simple. Indeed, one current theory states that any part of the brain contains all of the mind.

The brain, according to this theory, is like a *hologram*. When a laser is shot through a hologram plate, it projects a three-dimensional image of whatever has been caught within the plate. However, it is the hologram's other major characteristic that is of interest to the brain researcher. If you break a hologram up into small pieces, you can take any one of those pieces and put it in a laser's pathway. The result is the full image of the entire hologram. Every part of the hologram plate contains the complete image of that whole plate.

So it is with the brain and the mind. The brain is the hologram plate, the mind the hologram image. Take any part of the brain, and you have the complete mind. An intriguing idea, but how do you test it? Enter Paul Pietsch of Indiana University. Pietsch decided that the only way to test the *hologramic brain* theory was to scramble some animal's brain and see if it affected its basic behavior. Since such scrambling would kill most animals, he chose to work with the immature, aquatic form of the salamander (very similar to the tadpole, an immature frog) (see Figure 2). Salamanders not only can regrow neural tissue but also can survive all sorts of disruptions of their tiny brains.

But, even if Pietsch succeeds in showing that a salamander's brains can be scrambled without losing the basic character of its mind, how can we transfer that knowledge to the human brain? Can we really say that what is true of a salamander's brain, a rat's brain, or a cat's brain is true of a human brain? Well, any such inference is clearly that, an inference. We must realize that, until we can put any theory of the human brain's operation to the test, we can only say it might be that way, not that it absolutely is.

Still, Dr. David Hubel responds to this question by observing, "Our understanding of the brain is at such a level that there really aren't very great differences between the cat's and human's brain. The human brain is bigger, but then, there is more of us. Most of the parts that make up our brain are there in the cat. The human has more cortex and more parts to that cortex. But that's just one subdivision of the brain. The rest is there in the same amount and probably does the same thing."

So, what did Pietsch find? Is there a hologramic mind? Apparently yes. Pietsch began simply by just cutting out parts of the young salamander's brain, replacing each section with parts of the spinal cord. Thus, only part of the brain remained. According to Pietsch, these salamander young have two behavior responses. If it's larger than they are, they run away. If smaller, and it moves, they eat it. Pietsch's scrambled-brain salamanders fed just as readily and just as hungrily as those with whole brains. He had not destroyed the basic feeding habit.

Pietsch then began a complicated series of trials. He would take the cerebral hemispheres, reverse them in some animals, turn them upside-down in others, and exchange them with the back part of the brain in others. The salamanders continued to eat.

Not satisfied that he was showing the brain to be hologramic, he transplanted part of the brain of one species of salamander into the brain case of another. But, it wasn't just a straight transplant; Pietsch put the brain in without removing the other brain. Still the salamanders ate without any apparent ill effect on their behavior.

Pietsch's final test was to place the brain of a tadpole into one of the young salamanders. Later examination showed that the brain segment from the tadpole fused with the nervous system of the young salamander. Tadpoles are vegetarians, unlike young salamanders which are meat eaters. The salamanders with tadpole brains no longer would eat other animals. They had now, from the fragment of tadpole brain, become vegetarians.

Transplanting the Mind

The idea of transplanting memory or ability from one person to another is not a new idea, but the techniques for such a transplant are fairly new. Indeed, the same surgical procedures that allow for the neural grafts discussed in Chapter 6 should be applicable here. Such a neural transplant would "probably be easier than trying to do a liver or a lung transplant or something like that," says J. Eric Holmes. "I think the brain is going to have less trouble with rejection than a lot of other organs turn out to."

Elizabeth Loftus of the University of Washington doesn't think that the idea of a memory bank is so far-fetched. In the future, if you aren't satisfied with your own memories, you will go to a memory bank and have a new set grafted into your mind. Or perhaps you wish to forget a recent tragedy, go to the memory bank.

Dr. Holmes asks us to "imagine what would have happened if Einstein had died when we had a real good, neural tissue culture system. Instead of pickling his brain, as was done, we could have cultured it. We are on the verge of finding ways of implanting chunks of that culture into somebody who needs it." Those abilities, those talents which we thought lost forever, might be kept and passed from generation to generation. Do we need a solution to a problem in physics? Ask Einstein or Planck by implanting a part of each's mind in a contemporary physicist's brain.

Or perhaps the world faces a political crisis. Transplant tissues from those leaders who had to face a similar crisis in their day. Give modern leaders the perspective of others' decisions, not the bare, recorded testament of history, but the actual living memory with all of the dilemmas and actual thoughts of past leaders right there to be not just seen and heard, but experienced by the present.

Paul Pietsch may even have the evidence that such memory transplants are possible. Indeed, if his hologramic brain theory is correct, any segment of the brain should provide the source for any memory a person might desire. If salamander young with tadpole brain segments can turn from being carnivores, why not transplant the memory of one salamander into another? Pietsch tried this very experiment. He had two different species of salamander young in his lab. One set had been trained to respond to feeding by a flick of the finger against the side of their container. The other set fled from such an action. Pietsch put part of the brain of the trained lot into the brain of the runners. After they revived consciousness, the runners now would respond to the flick of a finger against the glass side. They no longer ran.

Memory and learning are still elusive quantities of the mind, but the neuroresearchers seem to have a good start down that road. Indeed, Dr. Holmes feels that "Memory may yield to a lot of routine cellular biochemistry. It may yield a lot of information to the implanted microelectrode. The Hubel-Wiesel technique of 'what's that single cell doing' that worked very well in the visual system."

8

Overcoming the Physical: Mind over Matter

With our minds we shape our world, perhaps not to our complete satisfaction and certainly not always with wisdom. But it is the application of our intelligence, our ability to reason and to discover and use relationships—all characteristics of our minds—that have allowed us to have a world closer to our desires and needs. No longer is the southern United States periodically devastated by floods; the dams of the TVA see to that. No longer do we have to fear polio and smallpox; medicine has seen to that. No longer does every family have to spend most of its day hunting and growing food just to survive; farm machinery and management have seen to that.

But is our intelligence the only feature of our minds that allows us to control and manipulate the world around us? No, that manipulation, that pushing around physical reality to meet our needs, is more complex than we have supposed in the past. Not all of these avenues being explored will prove to be real, and some may not at first glance appear to be what we are looking for, but, ultimately, our minds will give us the new tools—the mental tools—which will complement and aid the old physical tools.

The Mind's Other Senses

Ever since Rhine's experiments with extrasensory perception, ESP, in the 1930's and 1940's, the public imagination has been caught by claims of mind-reading ability, foreseeing the future, and moving objects with the mind. Each of these supposed abilities of the mind:

telepathy, clairvoyance, and *telekinesis* has been tested, as have many are those who claim to possess one or more of these talents.

How good is the evidence for such powers? Poor in too many cases. Much of what passes for psychic ability are tricks that professional magicians have known for centuries. James Randi, the Great Randi, has spent the last several years showing the tricks used by such frauds. He has a standing offer of ten thousand dollars for anyone who can demonstrate true psychic ability. So far, no one has claimed the prize. Randi does not say he disbelieves in psychic powers. He claims to have an open mind. All he asks for is proof, proof under good, sound conditions. He wants to know that he isn't seeing a trick.

Part of the problem believers in psychic phenomena have had is that they have not been able to provide the rigidly controlled scientific conditions good, hard scientific data need. Nor have they had much success in providing the repeatability necessary. Further, Randi feels that, even when skeptical observers such as scientists do monitor psychic demonstrations, they do not have the knowledge of professional magical tricks to help them spot hoaxes. He feels, therefore, that, with his professional knowledge, if he can be convinced, then psychic abilities may have some basis in truth.

The skepticism of Randi and others, however, has not diminished either the strength of belief in or the search to define and prove such talents. Indeed, the 1970's were in many ways the era of the psychic. We read about psychics helping the police find the sites of violent crimes, following the trails of victims of crimes. We hear of the ABC network employing a psychic to predict which shows will or will not succeed, and we read of psychics using their supposed abilities at archaeological sites to tell scientists where to dig for artifacts. Are these people actually demonstrating that they can do these things, or are they merely good guessers and good, convincing storytellers? Are they just good at deducing from subtle clues that people around them miss?

Certainly scientists such as J.B. Rhine and the physicist Helmut Schmidt feel there is some validity to telepathy, clairvoyance, and telekinesis. Both men attempted to test for such abilities. And, indeed, wouldn't it be pleasant if telekinesis or, as it is also known, *psychokinesis* (PK) were an unsuspected talent in each of us. No longer would we have to get out of our chairs to get a glass of water. Rather we could use the force of our mind to fill the glass from the faucet and bring it from the kitchen. We could mow the lawn with PK while finishing our homework. We could double, perhaps triple, the number of jobs we could do, thus saving ourselves time we could spend relaxing. Certainly PK would be an extremely useful tool. Even proponents of the existence of PK do not claim, however, that everyone has it. And even those who supposedly do have it, can only do fairly simple, nonexacting tasks such as rolling a pencil across a table. Still, if it does exist, perhaps, it can be brought out in everyone and strengthened through training.

But what is the evidence? Rhine tested for PK by asking his volunteer to affect the roll of a single die. The die would be thrown fifty or one hundred times. The subject would be asked generally to concentrate on rolling a six. At first, the die was thrown by one of the researchers. Later, a die-throwing machine was developed. Rhine got some results that seemed to indicate that six was coming up more often than it would normally be expected. The results were not spectacular, and the experiment had some basic faults that even someone who believes in PK such as Stephen E. Braude saw.

First, in pitted dice, the side with the six is the lightest, and will come face up more than the other sides. Second, no human hand can throw dice in a completely random fashion; the person's wrist will always twist or his fingers twitch in a certain manner so that a particular throw will be more likely to appear than others. Even a machine cannot be trusted to lack such a mechanical bias in throwing. Finally, as Braude points out, the whole physics of the movement of dice is so complex that no one can know if dice can be thrown randomly.

Without randomness, any results become meaningless. The differences between the expected and the supposed influence by PK is so small that any other contributing factor can eliminate the proof. What was needed then was a completely random test, in which any difference had to be a result of the application of PK. So, Helmut Schmidt developed the *random number generator* (RNG). The RNG has a pointer that moves between two positions, one labeled heads (+1) and one labeled tails (−1). The pointer switches back and forth between the two positions randomly a million times a second. The pointer is powered by the decay of the radioactive isotope Strontium-90 (SR-90). Radioactive decay is not easily influenced and certainly not by temperature or electromagnetic fields.

PK subjects try to get the pointer to move more times to one position or the other. Thus, a subject would see if he could get tails (−1) to be the pointer's target more than fifty percent of the time, as it would be without any outside influence. Schmidt's first test used fifteen randomly selected people. He did not try to find people with supposed PK ability. Most of the results showed tails dominating the test results. Schmidt then took the highest scoring subjects and had them repeat their tests. This time the negative score was larger, and Schmidt claimed that the odds against the scores was 1,000 to 1.

After this Schmidt developed a more complex RNG, the binary RNG. He found that his subjects could influence both RNG's equally well and to the same extent. Oddly enough, he also claimed that when the subjects did not try to influence the results, they were most successful in affecting the RNG's.

Does this mean that PK is now a proven fact? Not necessarily. It is difficult to find a complete description of Schmidt's methods, and, without that, we cannot be sure just how well he took into account all possible factors that would produce his results. Further, a third more complex test, failed to show PK in the same subjects tested above. So the questions still remain.

Unfortunately, the frauds do as well. James Randi has encountered many people who claim to have PK. And not one of them can pass Randi's test. The trick is always there. There is the young man who can turn the pages of the phone book with his mind. Randi showed that this can be done by merely blowing at just the right angle across the page. There is Uri Geller who could "bend spoons with his mind." As Randi points out, this is a very old stage magician's trick.

Whatever the eventual outcome of the psychic upsurge of the latter half of the twentieth century, this is one area in which fraud is easily perpetuated. Belief can be a fine thing, but gullibility has never proven anything. It is generally a serious liability for serious recognition.

Biofeedback

If control of the world around us by our mind, whether with PK or other psychic abilities, is far from a certainty, our minds' control of our bodies is not. We do not even think about the exact control we have over the voluntary muscles of our bodies. We sit and walk, move our arms, pick up things, and put them down. However, other functions of our body such as our heartbeat, blood pressure, hormonal flow, digestion, and so on do not seem to respond to conscious control. Or at least, Western medicine thought so until comparatively recently. All of these "involuntary" responses are overseen by a portion of the nervous system called the *autonomic nervous system.*

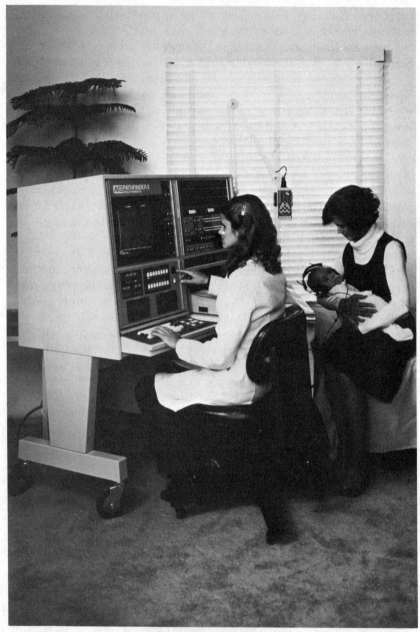

In the future, monitors such as this Nicolet Instruments Pathfinder II may be used to monitor body problems so that they may be treated through biofeedback. (Courtesy Nicolet Biomedical Instruments)

Yet we have all heard of yogis who can control their heart rates. Supposedly, in some cases, these men can stop their hearts and then restart them. Such men seem to have control over the autonomic nervous system. And indeed they do.

Elmer and Alyce Green at the Menninger Clinic in Topeka, Kansas, monitored such a yogi, Swami Rama, the head of the Himalayan Institute, headquartered in Pennsylvania. They discovered that this man could indeed control the rate of his heartbeat. However, when Swami Rama was asked to stop his heart, his heart rate, which had been 70, went up to 300 beats per minute. Instead of stopping the heart, the yogi speeded it up so much that the chambers did not fill completely and the heart valves did not work properly. The effect gave the illusion of the heart stopping. Still, the important fact was the conscious control on the yogi's part. Other yogis have shown they could lower their heart rate from 60 beats per minute to 30.

If these men could do it, then surely others could also. And with modern instrumentation, particularly EEG's, techniques have been developed to teach such control to sufferers of high blood pressure, asthma, epilepsy, tension headaches, migraines, chronic pain, and even stuttering. This control is accomplished through *biofeedback*. To understand the concept of feedback, think of a thermostat in a house. The thermostat controls the temperature in the house by telling the furnace either to turn on or off. You set the thermostat for 70 degrees. The house is 60 degrees, and the furnace comes on. The heat builds up until it is over 70 degrees. The thermostat tells (feeds back to) the furnace to turn off. The temperature falls until it is under 70 degrees and the thermostat tells (feeds back to) the furnace to turn back on. In this way, the thermostat regulates the temperature of the house, keeping it a fairly constant temperature.

Similarly our minds, like the thermostat, feed back to parts of our bodies to keep them operating at the required rate. If we are sitting or sleeping, our minds feed back to our hearts so that the heart rate is fairly slow. When we get up and start walking or running, our minds feed back to our hearts, raising the heart rate to meet the demand of the increased activity.

Biofeedback is the method by which we can tell our hearts to beat faster, our blood pressure to drop, or our headache to cease. How does it work? Well, take a sufferer of high blood pressure. He is hooked up to a machine that measures his blood pressure. Anytime his blood pressure decreases to safe levels, a light flashes in his eyes. Sometimes a pleasant picture such as a country scene will accompany the flashing light as a reward. This person's mind is being conditioned so that every time he sees the light flash he associates it with lowered blood pressure. After a time, the person will, when shown a flashing light, automatically lower his blood pressure. Oddly enough, the person does not have to have conscious control. Indeed, many do not feel that they are having any effect whatever. Yet the fact remains that people who have gone through this biofeedback training can and do control their blood pressure.

Obviously, a flashing light is not very practical. But other methods of alerting the person can work. A blood pressure monitor can be linked to a small earphone taped just behind a person's ear. When the blood pressure rises too high, the monitor sends a beep, and the mind takes over, lowering the pressure.

What else can biofeedback do besides help control blood pressure? Let us look at another role the mind plays and see how biofeedback comes in. There is no evidence that the mind is involved with most sickness, but at times, it does seem to be an important factor. Every doctor has seen patients whose complaint is a product of his or her mind. Such people show no actual physical disorder, but they insist they are suffering from everything from the flu to chronic back pains. Such illnesses are called *psychosomatic*. They are a product of the patient's mind. Indeed, they exist nowhere else but in that mind, certainly not in the body.

But not all such illnesses are so innocent. Sometimes, a person will convince his body that it really is sick. In that case, the symptoms can become very real and very deadly. Jim Kunzman, a Colorado farmer, suddenly developed cancer. His children had recently been killed in an automobile accident, and Kunzman's cancer followed almost on the heels of this tragedy. Chemotherapy didn't seem to have any effect upon Kunzman's condition. It only made him sick. Kunzman then started seeing a psychologist. He told the man about his feelings of utter loss from the death of his children and the void it had created in his life. As he talked, his sense of loss grew less, and he began to be interested in life once more. His cancer disappeared. There was no doubt that Kunzman had had cancer. Nor was there any question that he no longer had it.

At the Cancer Counseling Research Center in Fort Worth, Dr. Stephanie Matthews-Simonton and her husband, Dr. Carl Simonton, have studied a number of cancer cases. Some have been cured through a process similar to Kunzman's. The two doctors discovered that those whose cancer cleared up had had some tragedy in their lives just prior to the diagnosis for cancer. Also, these people were characterized by a weak will to live and an inability to let anger or

Routine monitoring of AEP's may one day be used for biofeedback training. (Courtesy Nicolet Biomedical Instruments)

resentment out. But psychological therapy was able to help a good many of these cancer patients.

The Simontons felt that biofeedback ought to work for more than just the system that controlled the heart and circulatory system. Why not the system that fought disease? So they had their cancer patients try biofeedback. They would tell the patient to think of a pleasant country scene. The patient did this three times a day. Eventually, the patient would be able to sense the cancer tumor. The Simontons then told him to will his body's defenses to attack the tumor. In most cases, the patient was able to do so successfully.

Training then may someday help each of us to make better use of our body's disease-fighting mechanisms. No one claims that such techniques will eliminate sickness or that it will be one hundred percent effective. But, in many cases, a person can apparently help his body, through his mind, rout what might otherwise be a dangerous disorder.

Most modern biofeedback also is done in connection with readouts from electrodes. These electrodes monitor the body and tell the patient what is wrong. The patient then concentrates on that particular problem, whether it be a simple cold or a serious heart ailment.

END SLEEPLESS NIGHTS
FOREVER

Have problems sleeping at nights? Tried those non-prescription drugs? They didn't work? Hot milk? No? Perhaps, you should try biofeedback.

That is just what is being done in Tokyo. Researchers have found that one of the major elements in the lie detector test can be used to help insomniacs fall asleep. Lie detectors measure the conductivity of the skin, which tells the machine how alert the person being questioned is.

These skin conductivity readings are run through an instrument that allows insomniacs to decrease the conductivity of their skin and consequently their alertness by lowering the volume of ocean sounds. Done in a dark room, the problem sleepers generally soon find themselves asleep.

Skin conductivity's relationship to alertness will also be used to help keep people awake when they drive. The readings are rigged to an alarm system. If the driver's alertness falls below a certain level, showing he is drifting off to sleep, the alarm sounds.

The idea here is to give the mind as sharp a focus as possible, so that it doesn't waste its energy on unimportant or distracting information.

Tom Budzynski, director of the Biofeedback Institute, hopes that, in the future, we will all have wristwatch-sized body monitors. Every morning, we would check our monitor. It would tell us what we should concentrate on correcting that day. Perhaps you are nervous about a big meeting that day. Stress is building. You would, using biofeedback, try to ease tense muscles and lower blood pressure. You might do this by controlling the level of adrenaline in your blood. You could keep enough of this hormone flowing so you had the necessary "edge" to see you easily through the meeting, but not so much that it was damaging to your body.

NASA is working on a biofeedback monitor to help combat zero-G sickness. Queasiness plagued the crew on the third space shuttle mission. In the future, astronauts would swallow a microscopic monitor. This monitor would register the first symptoms of zero-G nausea. The astronaut could then begin consciously controlling his body's response. The problem would be over, easier and cheaper than drugs with no physical side effects.

You can buy an inexpensive biofeedback device at some electronic equipment stores. The biofeedback device works like a lie detector—increasing the conductivity of your skin by increasing sweat production. (Sweat is acidic, and acidic skin conducts a small current better than dry skin.)

Dreams

We normally do not think of dreams as a tool to deal with our world, to change it. But in many ways they are. On one level, in our dreams we change our world to something different than that which we see every day. We do so to deal with our problems. It has become a cliché in the latter half of the twentieth century that dreaming is the mind's way of working out its problems and relieving its frustrations. You have been having a hard time in one of your subjects at school. The final exam is tomorrow so you dream that you are unable to find your sister in a large department store. You don't even know why you have to find her. But if you don't, something bad will happen. Your dream dissolves into a welter of strange, unformed faces, but none of them is your sister. The quest for your sister represents the struggle you have been having learning that subject. You must have mastery of it tomorrow, or you will fail the test. You are still feeling confused by all the facts you have learned, just as in your dream you are surrounded by those strange, half-formed faces. The certainty you need to do well on the test is as elusive as the sister you never find in the dream.

The relationship between dreams and the real world has puzzled and fascinated humanity for tens of thousands of years. Our ancestors, until comparatively recently, saw them as often prophetic, showing what was to come. Indeed, there are people today who still view dreams as clairvoyant visions. Modern dream theory, however, really starts with the publication of Sigmund Freud's *The Interpretation of Dreams* (1899). Freud had become interested in the value of dreams in analyzing the problems of his patients and had found that dreams often gave him some good clues to approaches for treatment. To Freud, dreams represented repressed feeling, particularly sexual, the things that most people did not wish to recognize or discuss. The dream was a safety valve for these feelings. Also, the successful dream did not intrude on the waking life of the person, but rather to Freud, dreams were guardians that kept the person safely asleep while working through the feelings they represented.

Freud's ideas on dreams, although certainly worthy, were too limited for one of his disciples, Carl Jung. Dreams represented for Jung more than erotic urges that should be recognized and accepted by the conscious self, not just the sleeping self. Perhaps, Jung's most interesting theory about dreams was his claim that they linked each of us with what he called the collective unconscious of the race. Jung postulated that the many common elements found in everyone's dreams allowed each of us to share a common racial experience. These elements, which Jung called *archetypes,* not only appear in dreams, but also in all human myths. Thus, we all dream about concepts such as creation, paradise, the mother and father figures, and the monster in some form or other. For Jung, the symbols in each person's dream were unique in one sense to that person. The symbols, although they might represent one or more archetypes, also stood for facets unique to the dreamer's own life. Therefore, we gain an understanding of ourselves by analyzing our dreams, and what we learn is for ourselves.

Modern dream theory goes along with Jung to a great extent. An expert such as Montague Ullman sees our dreams as a method of exploring the emotional impact of recent events in our lives. Often, particularly when something bad has happened, the dream becomes a healing mechanism. So, our mind with the dream can and does heal psychological scars much as it can, with biofeedback, heal physical scars.

But the idea of biofeedback is control. Can we gain such control over our dreams? Can we create our own future selves or must we go whichever way our dreams take us whether we wish to go there or not? Some researchers, such as Stephen LaBerge of Stanford University, say no. LaBerge is one of many psychologists studying the control of *lucid dreams*. These are dreams which are very vivid and in which you know you are dreaming. According to studies over the last decade, some ten percent of us can stop in the middle of such a dream, look around, decide this isn't the right dream, and change it.

You are dreaming. Walking around a corner, you meet a street gang. They are almost a formless menace, but you have no doubt they intend at best to rough you up. At worst . . . . You know you are dreaming, and you feel particularly helpless. Suddenly, you say, "Enough." You walk over to the gang's leader and offer to shake hands. "Let's talk," you say. "Sure, man," he says. You all sit down right there and everyone tells everyone else about what he wants and is unable to get. The nightmare is over because you altered its course.

Of course, matters are not so simple. Not everyone has the ability to change his dreams. At least not yet. LaBerge's research does seem to show that the ability can be learned. If so, the future of our nights may be far different than the past.

The neuroscientists have only begun charting the shoals and reefs of the mind. What the safe harbors and landfalls are still mostly a matter of conjecture. And the nature of that land of the mind is only glimpsed through the exploration of dreaming and hallucinations.

What is intelligence? What controls it? Can we learn to control it? These are questions that have no answers yet. Indeed, many feel that even the questions have not yet really been asked.

Ultimately, it is technique that is needed. For J. Eric Holmes, the search for consciousness, intelligence, memory, learning, dreaming, all the areas of the mind "is waiting for someone to come along with a new technique. Then, it will light up again and get real exciting. I don't know, of course, what that technique will be."

But, when it arrives, the exploration of the mind will probably be the greatest adventure of all. For our minds are us, and we are our world.

9

Reaching Beyond Our Horizon: The Future Brain

Brain-Computer Link

Your boss has assigned you to determine the feasibility of manufacturing solar energy screens. You know nothing about solar energy and even less about solar energy screens.

You have two hours to present the whole package to your boss. Are you worried? No. It will be a cinch. After your presentation, she orders production to start immediately.

Later that night, you sit down in your favorite chair and decide to watch TV. The images form in your mind. Later, while you are going to sleep, music plays softly through your mind from your favorite radio station. The volume decreases as you drift asleep, stopping completely as your brain waves fall into the sleep pattern.

The next day, you silently place an order with your autochef for bacon and eggs. Another thought programs the house's cleaning unit to vacuum and dust. You look outside and notice that the ultraviolet is particularly intense today. You put on some sunscreen before going for your morning run. As you run, you keep track of your heart rate, breathing, and muscle tension. When each reaches a certain level, you turn around and return home. You have had the maximum benefit from your exercise.

How was all this done? Through a direct brain-computer hookup: A computer, the size of a circuitry chip, has been implanted in the back of your head.

This computer allows you to have access to any information network in the world, from the Library of Congress to the Congressional Record. Want to know about solar energy? Your computer pulls everything needed. The computer also will be able to receive from, and transmit to, your brain's TV and radio signals. It will allow you to send electric messages to your household appliances, monitor your body's functions, and even see various forms of radiation that are now invisible.

Nor is that all. Through your computer, you will be able to talk directly with the mind of any other computer wearer. Telepathy will be a reality, and our society—our world—will change. What it will become, we do not know. But it will be different.

Is this science fiction? Not according to Glenn Cartwright of McGill University. Although we are not yet able to connect a computer to the human brain and have the two communicate with one another, the first steps have already been taken. Recently, the Air Force funded a project to see if a computer could be controlled by the mental activity of a man. A volunteer was hooked up to an EEG. This in turn was connected to a radio transmitter. The man was able then to modulate his alpha waves so that he could send a Morse code signal through the radio via the EEG. On the receiving end of the radio was a computer. The signal was able to instruct the computer to do simple tasks.

Although this kind of control is limited and the equipment bulky, clearly the human brain can communicate directly with a computer. According to Cartwright, the eventual brain-computer hookups will be called symbionic minds. (*Sym* for symbiosis, when two organisms live together to their mutual benefit; *bionic* for the combination of machine and living organism.)

The key to such a link will be the EEG research of today. The computer will have to be able to respond to electrical activity in the brain, particularly that which conveys a direct question or request to the computer. If the work with P300 and the mapping of electrical patterns we saw in Chapter 3 brings us a code to understand the meaning of the electrical activity in our brains, then we have the essential element to create the symbionic mind.

The only other real problem will be linking the slower electrical activity of the human brain to the incredibly faster activity of the computer—some billion times faster than that of human neurons. However, this stepping down of the computer response time to match the human is already practical.

Brain Transplant

Since 1962, organ transplants have become more and more commonplace. Heart transplants still receive the bulk of the publicity, but kidney and lung transplants are just as practical and just as safe. Transplanting the brain is another of the future prospects.

How soon can we expect such transplants? J. Eric Holmes believes that "transplanting the entire brain from one head to the other is surgically possible now. Some years back, a neurosurgeon was doing a complete removal of the brain of animals, keeping the blood supply on a pump, taking away the entire skull, and putting the brain in a nutrient bath. He kept it alive for several days. The brain continued producing EEG and could use oxygen and glucose. That's the first step—getting it out without destroying it."

Dr. Holmes goes on to say that placing the brain in a donor body is probably practical with today's microsurgical techniques. The real problem is keeping the brain alive during the transfer. Dr. Holmes feels that some sort of suspended animation—lowering the body temperature of both body and brain—would be crucial for the success of the operation. Such suspended animation would lower the rate of the chemical processes in both body and brain and would lengthen life sufficiently to allow time for the whole operation.

Then comes the most difficult part.

"When you've done all that, you're confronted with the problem," continues Dr. Holmes, "of how to get the axons in the transplanted brain to grow out and make connections with what's left of the host's nervous system or muscular system or whatever. At the moment, that's what really prevents attempts to transplant brains. Nobody knows how to get those axons to grow."

Despite this problem, Dr. Holmes says, "It turns out that there are places in the hippocampus and elsewhere where you can show that cut axons do just that—regrow. So, it should be possible for us to do it. That's the breakthrough we need. A way to get the new brain to connect to the old spinal cord and activate it and move the muscles and see with the optic nerve or whatever."

Senile Dementia

Until recently, we have assumed that among older people, some will inevitably become senile. They no longer can remember things well. They think poorly. They become more and more childlike.

What we call *senile dementia* is really Alzheimer's disease. It generally strikes people after their middle sixties, but it can hit people as young as their middle forties. Although Alzheimer's disease is now incurable, neuroscientists are hoping to develop a vaccine against the disease. We would all be vaccinated at birth, and as J. Eric Holmes says, "almost nobody would suffer a decline in intellect and personality as they got older. We would all be bright as a tack as we got to be eighty or ninety. The only thing that would kill us is when our other systems gave out."

An Ending for a Beginning

The future of brain research will probably be as surprising and unexpected as the knowledge we have today might seem to scientists of the past. Any discipline that draws the attention of such a variety of investigators—from biologists to doctors, from psychologists to philosophers and linguists, from computer scientists and physicists to engineers and mathematicians—is for a time confused and hectic. But with such a variety of approaches, the findings must come, and the picture of what the brain is must also eventually gel. All the models of today will one day give way to *the* model of tomorrow.

What good will this all do us? The medical and psychological solutions to physical and mental disease should be enough justification, but if more is needed, let us listen to Alan Gevins, one of the researchers:

"I think it's probable we haven't yet figured out how to use our frontal lobes to their full capacity. We have the hardware, but not the software. The capacity or potential is there, but the programs haven't been written yet. There are massive fiber tracts that lead from the frontal lobes to the limbic system. These are control tracts.

"If we found out through education and training how to more optimally make use of our frontal lobes and the rest of our brains, it is possible that some of the animalistic behavior we engage in now, such as killing each other, might be eliminated. Study of the brain is one of the few things around that actually might make a difference."

Selected Reading List

Asimov, Isaac. *The Human Brain.* Houghton Mifflin, 1963.

Blakeslee, Thomas R. *The Right Brain.* Doubleday, 1980.

Carr, Donald E. *The Forgotten Senses.* Doubleday, 1972.

Gluhbegovic, Nedzad and Terreance H. Williams. *The Human Brain: A Photographic Guide.* Harper & Row, 1980.

Restak, Richard M. M.D. *The Brain: The Last Frontier.* Doubleday, 1979.

Rosenfeld, Albert, ed. *Mind and Supermind.* Holt, 1977.

Scientific American's The Brain (reprint of September 1979 issue), 1980.

Stevens, Leonard A. *Explorers of the Brain.* Knopf, 1971.

Glossary

Acetylcholine. The chemical that carries the nerve impulse across the synapse from one neuron to the next.

ACTH (Adrenocorticotrophic hormone). Part of the peptide that contains endorphin; it stimulates the adrenal glands to produce adrenaline.

Alpha waves. Represent the brain's readiness for action.

Amino acids. Chemical building blocks of proteins and peptides, in addition to carbon, hydrogen, and oxygen, contain nitrogen.

Arachnoid membrane. The second of the three layers surrounding and protecting the brain.

Archetype. Jung's concept of common mythic symbols shared by all people that link them to a racial collective unconscious.

Autonomic nervous system. That part of the nervous system which controls such "involuntary" functions as heart rate, blood pressure, hormonal flow, etc.

Autoradiography. Exposure of a tissue sample containing a radioactive tracer to a strip of film to produce a photographic image.

Average evoked potential (AEP). Found by averaging the EEG readings from a whole series of trials using a specific stimulus.

Axon. A long, unbranched fiber, emerging from a neuron, that carries the nerve impulse away from the body of the cell toward the next neuron.

Beta-endorphin. See Endorphin.

Beta waves. Beta I, like alpha waves, show the brain's readiness for action; beta II show intense mental activity.

Biochemistry. The study of the chemical composition and chemical reactions of living organisms.

Biofeedback. Control by a person's mind of the functions under the regulation of the autonomic nervous system.

Brain pacemaker. An implanted device that sets up a counter current at the beginning of an epileptic seizure, thus effectively ending the attack.

Brain stem. One of the three major divisions of the brain responsible for monitoring muscular movement and also for receiving nerve impulses through the cranial nerves.

Brain waves. Recordings of changes in electrical potential from cells in the cerebrum.

Broca center. Language center in the left cerebral hemisphere that controls the ability to speak.

Carbon-11. A radioactive form of the carbon atom.

Cerebellum. One of the three major divisions of the brain responsible for muscular coordination.

Cerebral hemispheres. The two divisions of the cerebrum, labeled left and right.

Cerebrospinal fluid. A protective fluid in which the brain floats.

Cerebrum. One of the three major divisions of the brain composing some eighty per cent of the brain. It contains centers for sight, sound, smell, and touch; it also is the site for intelligence and memory.

Cholinesterase. The chemical that breaks down acetylcholine.

Chromosomes. Carriers of the genetic material DNA.

Clairvoyance. Being able to see things not in a person's presence.

Complex primary visual cortex cells.   Respond to a line in the field of vision only when it is at a specific angle; position does not matter.

Computerized axial tomography (CAT) scanner.   Uses X rays and computer assistance to present detailed images of sections of the brain.

Corpus callosum.   A bridge of fibers that allows the two cerebral hemispheres to communicate.

Cortex or Cerebral cortex.   The furrowed, outer surface of the cerebrum that carries out many cerebral functions.

Delta waves.   In adults, show the presence of brain damage or disorders.

Dendrites.   The branched extensions of the neuron that receive nerve impulses from other nerve cells.

2-Deoxyglucose.   Similar to glucose, but once entered into a cell, it is trapped.

d-lysergic acid diethylamide.   See LSD.

DNA.   The chemical that provides genetic information.

Dopamine.   A neurotransmitter that, when in excessive amounts in the limbic system, contributes to the development of schizophrenia and that, when in insufficient amounts in the cerebrum, causes Parkinson's disease.

Double mind or Double brain.   The two cerebral hemispheres, each of which has specialized functions. The left is basically verbal, the right spatial.

DPA (d-phenylalanine).   Stops the enzymatic breakdown of enkephalin.

Dura mater.   The outermost of the three membranes surrounding and protecting the brain.

Electrical potential.   The separation of positive and negative charges, voltage.

Electroencephalogram (EEG). Process of using scalp-attached electrodes to record changes in electric potential within the cerebral cortex, producing brain wave charts.

Electron. A negatively charged particle found in atoms.

Endorphin. One of the brain's natural opiates that is produced by the pituitary gland and is involved with pain control.

Enkephalin. One of the brain's natural opiates, involved with pain control.

Enzymes. Proteins and peptides that begin chemical reactions in the body and that are not consumed in the reaction.

Epilepsy. Seizures resulting from uncontrolled firing of neurons in either the motor or sensory area of the cerebrum.

Estrogen. The chemical that determines female sex.

Evoked potential or Evoked response. An EEG recording from a single, specific stimulus.

Field of vision. Everything that both human eyes can see when staring straight ahead.

Frontal lobes. The upper front section of the cerebral hemispheres.

Gamma rays. Given off by radioactive material when a positron collides with an electron.

Gland. A group of cells that produces one or more hormones.

Glial or Glia cells. One of the types of cells composing the brain that protect, support, and feed neurons.

Glucose. A sugar and the basic fuel for the cells of the human body.

Golgi method. A staining process that colors complete, single neurons.

Grand mal. The severest form of epilepsy.

Hippocampus. A structure located in the temporal lobes that may be the site of learning ability and decision making.

Hologram. Holds a three-dimensional image that is revealed when a laser passes through the plate. Also, any fragment of the plate will reveal the complete image.

Hologramic brain. The theory that any part of the brain contains the entire mind, just as any part of a hologram holds the entire image.

Hormone. A chemical produced and released by a gland that circulates through the bloodstream until it reaches its target cells, which it then stimulates into activity.

Hypercomplex primary visual cortex cells. Respond to a line of specific length that falls anywhere in the field of vision and that is at any angle.

Hypothalamus. Controls pleasure, body temperature, and sleep.

Ion. Formed when an atom either loses or gains one or more electrons.

Lateral geniculate bodies. The region of the brain into which the optic nerve first feeds its signal.

L-dopa. A dopamine-based chemical that can help keep Parkinson's disease in check.

Left brain. The left cerebral hemisphere, linked with verbal skills.

Limbic system. The bottom part of the cerebrum that controls emotions.

LSD. A synthetic compound, d-lysergic acid diethylamide, that produces schizophrenic-like symptoms.

Lucid dreams. Dreams that are very vivid and in which the person knows he or she is dreaming. Such dreams can be changed by the conscious control of some dreamers.

Manic-depression. A form of mental illness in which the victim swings between extremes of hyperactivity and deep depression.

Medulla oblongata. One of the three divisions of the brain stem.

Microelectrodes. Electrodes whose tips are small enough to slip into individual nerve cells.

Midbrain. One of the three divisions of the brain stem.

Motor area. Part of the cerebral cortex that controls the movement of the body.

Myelin sheath. A fatty layer that surrounds the neuron's axon.

Naloxone. A chemical which can bind to the opiate receptor sites instead of endorphin, but which has no pain-controlling ability.

Neomammalian. The outermost of Paul MacLean's triple brain, the cerebrum, and the location of conscious thought.

Nerve signal or impulse. The electrical messages carried by the neurons.

Neural graft. A transplant of neural tissue from a healthy, fetal brain to a section of damaged adult brain.

Neurobiology. The study of the biology of the brain.

Neurochemistry. The study of the chemical composition and chemical reactions of neurochemicals in the brain.

Neurohormone. A hormone that acts as a neurotransmitter.

Neurology. The study of the nervous system.

Neurometrics. A method for diagnosing brain disorders by comparing AEP's from several different regions of the brain with AEP's taken from normal, healthy human brains.

Neuron. The major cell making up the brain and nervous system that carries signals to and from the brain and performs much of the brain's work.

Neurotensin. Another painkilling neurotransmitter.

Neurotransmitter. A chemical that either turns on or turns off the activity of a neuron.

Non-invasive instruments. Machines such as the CAT and PETT scanners that allow the brain to be observed from outside the skull.

Nuclear magnetic resonance (NMR) scanner. An instrument that develops images from the biochemical operations of the brain with a magnetic field.

Occipital lobes. One of the rear sections of the cerebral hemispheres.

Ocular dominance columns. Cells in each of these columns, found in the primary visual cortex, process information from either the right eye or the left eye; there is no mixing of right-left eye information within columns.

Olfactory nerve. Carries impulses from the nose to the brain.

Opiates. The active elements in heroin, morphine, and opium, which are similar in structure to endorphins and enkephalins found naturally in the brain.

Optacon. A reading device for the blind.

Optic chiasm. The point at which the right and left optic nerves cross.

Optic nerve. Carries impulses from the eyes to the brain.

Orientation columns. Cells with each column are either simple, complex, or hypercomplex; there is no mixing of types of cells within the columns.

Paleomammalian. The second layer of Paul MacLean's triple brain, equivalent to the limbic system, and the seat of emotions.

Parietal lobes. One of the rear sections of the cerebral hemispheres.

Parkinson's disease. Results from injury of nerves controlling body movement and sensory input, marked by a gentle shaking of hands and head and a rigidity of face and arms.

Peptide. A long sequence of amino acids.

Petit mal. One of the gentlest forms of epilepsy.

Pia mater. The innermost layer of the membranes surrounding and protecting the brain.

Pituitary gland. Located just below the hypothalamus, produces many hormones as well as endorphin.

PK. See Psychokinesis.

Placebo. A pill or injection that contains no actual medicine, but which is given to patients who want more such medicine than is good for them.

Pons. One of the three divisions of the brain stem.

Positron. A positively charged electron.

Positron emission transaxial tomography (PETT) scanner. An instrument used to record and create images of the chemical activity in regions of the brain.

Primary visual cortex. Signals from the eyes are fed into this region of the brain from the lateral geniculate bodies, and it is where information from both eyes is first combined.

Pro-opiomelanocortin. The long peptide that contains both ACTH and endorphin.

Prosthesis. An artificial substitute for a missing or damaged body part.

Proton. A positively charged particle in an atom.

Psychokinesis. The ability to move objects with the force of the mind.

Psychosomatic illness. Illness which is a product of a person's mind and which shows no actual physical causes.

Random number generator. A device invented by Helmut Schmidt to test for psychokinesis. The test involves affecting the swing of a pointer between two positions, heads ($+1$) and tails (-1). The pointer's position is normally determined by the decay of Strontium-90.

R-complex. The innermost layer of Paul MacLean's triple brain, equivalent to the oldest part of the brain, controls instinctive behavior.

Receptor sites. Places on the neuron's dendrites at which various chemicals can fasten (bind) and initiate the nerve cell to action.

Retina. The back part of the eye that contains the light receptors and feeds into the optic nerve.

Right brain. The right cerebral hemisphere, linked with spatial skills.

RNG. See Random number generator.

Schizophrenia. A form of mental illness in which the sufferer withdraws from reality, often accompanied by hallucinations and feelings of persecution.

Sensory area. Part of the cerebral cortex that receives information from the skin.

Sensory substitution. Using one sense to feed information into a region of the brain that controls a defective sense such as using touch to replace sight.

Serotonin. A chemical that has been linked with schizophrenia.

Simple primary visual cortex cells. Respond to a line in the field of vision only if it is in a specific position and at a specific angle.

Stains. A chemical used to color tissue samples and individual cells for study.

Stimulation.   Exciting a response from a nerve receptor such as activating smell receptors with perfume or taste receptors with sugar.

Stimulus.   Anything such as a flashing light, the touch of a feather, the need to line up an arrow with a target, etc., that causes the brain to become active.

Substance P.   A neurotransmitter involved with the transmission of chemical pain.

Synapse.   The gap between the axon of one neuron and the dendrite of the next.

Tactile vision substitution system (TVSS).   A system by which stimulation of the skin is used to replace vision in the blind.

Telekinesis.   See Psychokinesis.

Telepathy.   Being able to read another's thoughts.

Temporal lobes.   Section of the cerebral hemispheres found on the side.

Testosterone.   The chemical that determines the male sex.

Thalamus.   Part of the brain that automatically responds to extremes in temperature and to pain.

Theta waves.   Commonly seen in children under five and generally only in adults suffering from extreme mental illness.

Tomogram.   A photograph of a section of skull and brain made by a computer for CAT or PETT scans.

Tomography.   The process of scanning through a single section of tissue and bone.

Tracers.   Radioactive compounds injected into a living body to allow doctors to trace their course through that body.

Triple brain.   Paul MacLean's concept of the brain as having three layers, the R-complex that controls instinct, the paleomammalian (the limbic system) that controls emotion, and the neomammalian (the cerebrum) that controls thought.

Tumor. An unnatural cellular growth that may be benign or malignant.

Tyrosine. An amino acid that has some role in controlling blood pressure.

Tritium. Radioactive form of hydrogen.

Wernicke center. Language center that allows us to speak sentences that make sense.

X ray. A form of radiation used to examine the interior of organisms.

Index